Skira**M**ini**ART**books

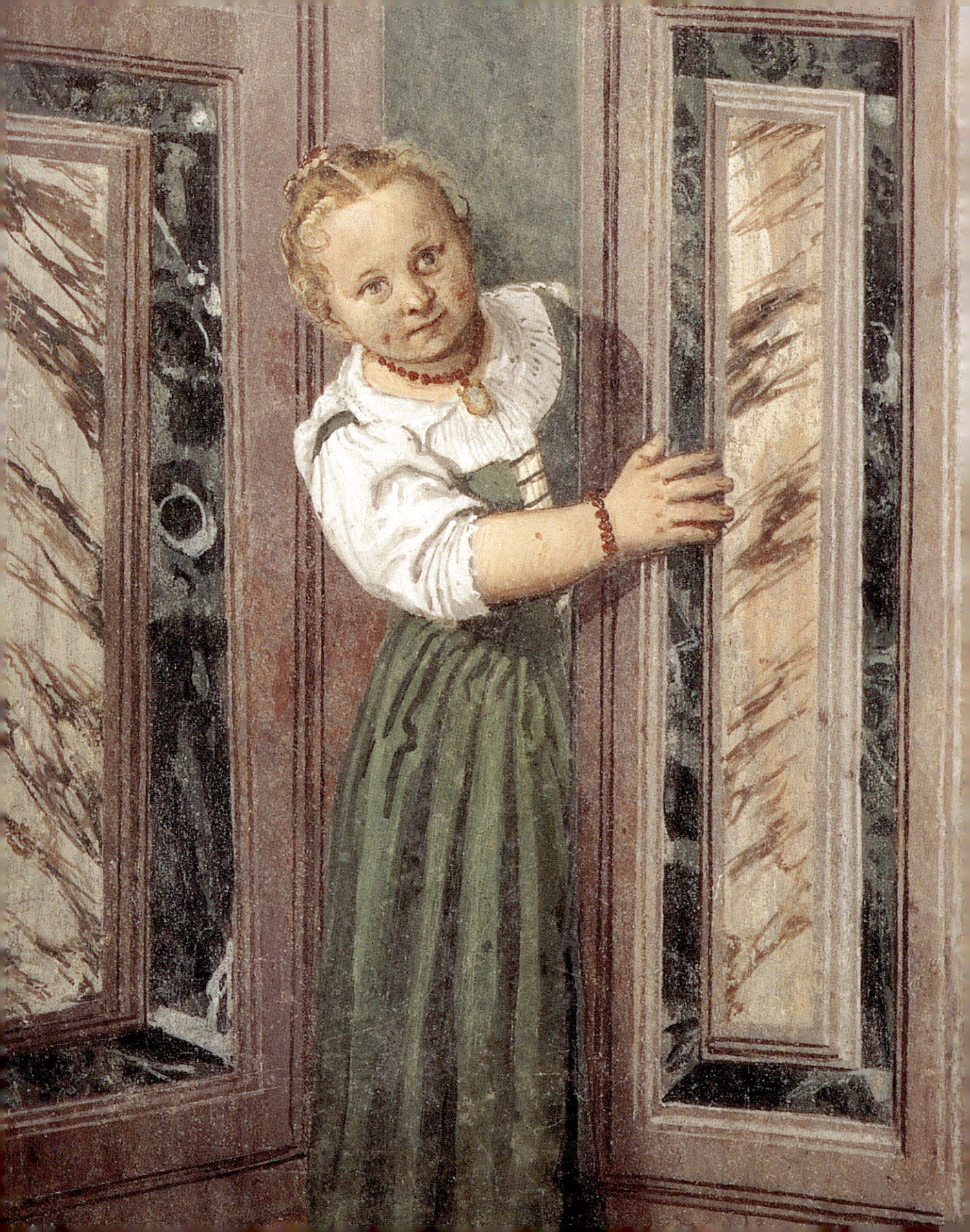

Flaminio Gualdoni

TROMPE L'OEIL

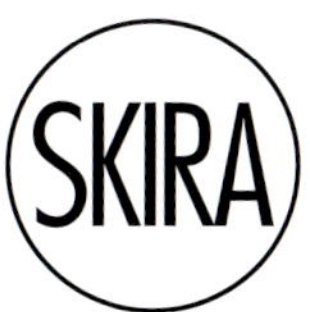

front cover
Giuseppe Maria Crespi
Shelves with music books
(detail), *circa* 1725
Oil on canvas
Civico Museo Bibliografico
Musicale, Bologna

Skira editore
SkiraMiniARTbooks

Editor
Eileen Romano

Design
Marcello Francone

Editorial Coordination
Giovanna Rocchi

Layout
Anna Cattaneo

Iconographical Research
Alice Spadacini

Editing
Maria Conconi

Translation
Robert Burns for Language
Consulting Congressi, Milan

First published in Italy in 2008
by Skira Editore S.p.A.
Palazzo Casati Stampa
via Torino 61
20123 Milano
Italy

www.skira.net

Printed and bound in Italy.
First edition

ISBN 978-88-6130-540-3

Distributed in North America by
Rizzoli International Publications,
Inc., 300 Park Avenue South,
New York, NY 10010.
Distributed elsewhere in the world
by Thames and Hudson Ltd.,
181a High Holborn, London
WC1V 7QX, United Kingdom.

facing title page
Paolo Veronese
Young girl
(detail of the decorative fresco
in the entrance hall), 1561-62
Fresco
Villa Barbaro, Maser

on page 90
Giovan Battista Lombardi
Dolente velata, 1856
Marble
Vantiniano cemetery, monument
to the Dossi-Rampinelli-Spalenza
family, Portico VI, Brescia

Contents

Trompe l'oeil

For centuries, the fundamental quality demanded of painting was the capacity to reproduce what we see with such fidelity that it ended up transforming into a bona fide art of deception.

This mindset was so entrenched that during the initial enthusiasm for the newly born technique of photography, Charles Baudelaire's opinion in his commentary *On Photography* from the Salon review of 1859—where he referred to photographers as "would-be painters (…) too lazy or ill-endowed to complete [their] studies"—caused an uproar when he criticised the medium for its "factual exactitude", for capturing reality exactly as it is, and asserted that the painter had a different, much higher and more complex calling. *Au contraire!*, responded contemporary opinion, photography's justification is to be found precisely in the human ambition to produce images that achieve an increasing resemblance to what we actually see. Hence, if anything, it is to be interpreted as the fulfilment of a quest for similitude that traces its roots back to the dawn of humanity. This is, if we look well, the same general opinion that applauded the unsettling yet captivating three-dimensionality of the hologram technique that won the Nobel prize for Dennis Gabor in 1971, and that now views the Internet-based *Second Life* as a sort of ultra-art.

In effect, there was more than one historical reason for the development and consolidation of an idea of painting as a virtuous counterfeiting of the real. Take for example the anecdote recounted by Pliny the Elder in his *Naturalis Historia* regarding Parrhasius, one of the recognised and celebrated genii of Greek art: "This last, it is said, entered into a pictorial contest with Zeuxis, who represented some grapes, painted so naturally that the birds flew towards the spot where the picture was exhibited. Parrhasius, on the other hand, exhibited a curtain, drawn with such singular truthfulness, that Zeuxis, elated with the judgment which had been passed upon his work by the birds, haughtily demanded that the curtain should be drawn aside to let the picture be seen. Upon finding his mistake, with a great degree of ingenuous candour he admitted that he had been surpassed, for that whereas he himself had only deceived the birds, Parrhasius had deceived him, an artist."

This tale, out of the dense repertory of Greco-Roman narrative, gave rise to an anecdotage that has been passed down through history regarding the incredible effects that can be achieved through skilled technique. For example, Vasari relates that during one of his travels, the artist Cimabue saw the shepherd "Giotto, who, while his sheep were grazing, had taken a flat, clean slab and, using a pointed stone, drawn a natural-looking sheep, with no other instruction than his natural instinct", with such ability that he would become the one who "gave rise to the modern and good art of painting, introducing the practice of portraying real people in their natural state."

The tale indicates that in effect, the great legacy of Greek painting, the pillar of Western art, is precisely the desire to deceive the eye of the beholder with an illusion of reality. Zeuxis, a Macedonian court painter cited as a grand master by Plato himself (in spite of the fact that the Greek philosopher considered perceived reality to be in itself a deception with respect to the higher and eternal truth), and Parrhasius, who has come down through history as the inventor of shading to suggest depth in the portrayed image, have become legendary figures in the arts. But alongside them we also have the *skiagraphia* of Apollodorus of Athens from the Classical Greek period, a painting style which, according to Pliny, "invented light and shad-

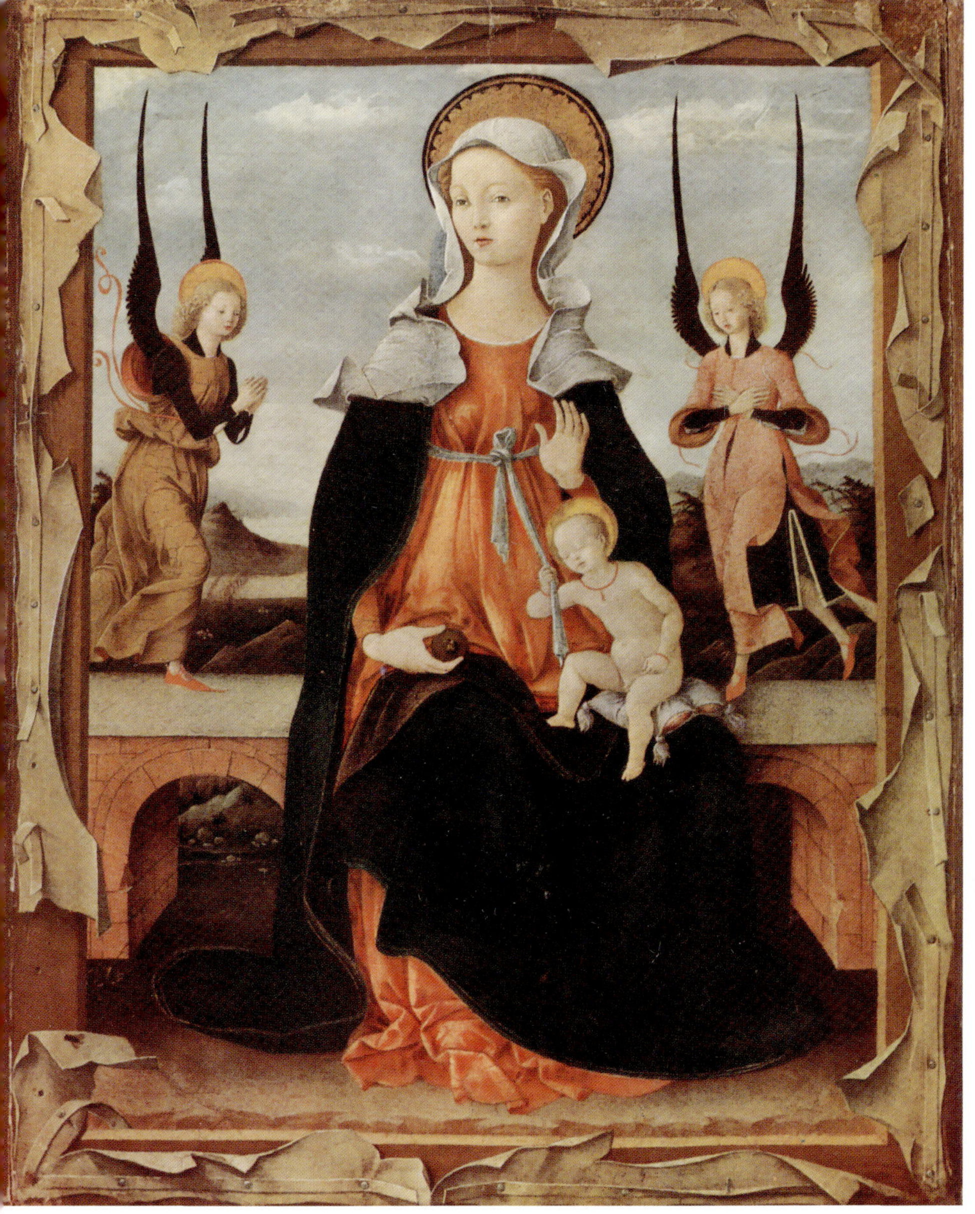

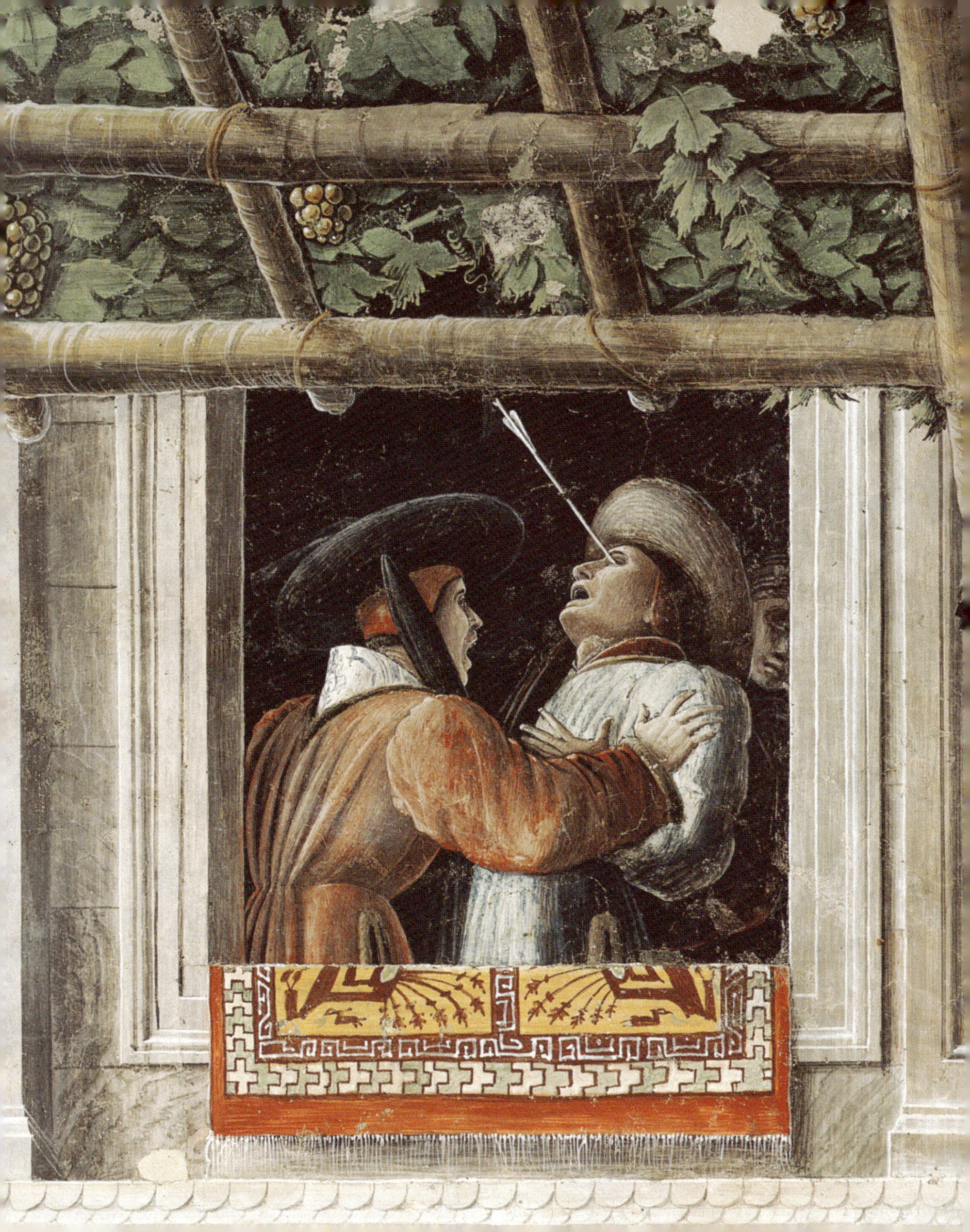

ow" and gave the first taste of perspective representation, and the illusionist scenography of Agatharkos, in which the spectators thought they were seeing architectural spaces that did not actually exist.

Nothing is left of their work, but we do have some strong indications in the wall paintings of Pompeii and Herculaneum, many of which were preserved in good condition in the aftermath of the eruption of Vesuvius in 79 AD, and in similar historical evidence unearthed in Rome.

The most elementary styles involved the imitation of variegated marble, alabaster or porphyry. In others we behold a triumph of fake architectural cloisters opening onto natural landscapes, or else garlands with birds and insects reproduced with astounding accuracy. And as a game within the illusionistic game, in some cases we have painting that deceptively depicts paintings hung on the wall: these are called *xenia*, the ancestors of our modern still-lifes.

The *xenia* were the "gifts for guests", fruit, bread, eggs, vegetables or jugs of milk that the host placed in the guests' rooms so that they would find nothing lacking. Quite soon the technique was adopted of painting pictures portraying those foods and placing them in the guest rooms, as a double or substitute for the real thing. As late as the 2nd century AD the scholar Philostratus the Elder, describing paintings such as these, guilefully suggested: "Why, then, do you not take the ripe fruit, of which there is a pile here in the other basket? Do you not know that in a little while you will no longer find it so fresh, but already the dew will be gone from it?" The illusionistically counterfeited paintings represent the splendid precursor to what would become a widespread practice in seventeenth and eighteenth-century European art.

11

After the close of the Roman period and the long season of the Middle Ages, the tradition of ancient art was revived thanks to Humanism. The ancient paintings from Rome and Pompeii had yet to be rediscovered, but the study of authors like Pliny and Cicero instilled anew the desire for an art that not only portrays faithfully, but pursues that faithfulness all the way into deception. Giovanni Boccaccio's estimation of Giotto is famous, that he was "a man of such outstanding genius that (…) whatever he depicted had the appearance, not of a reproduction, but of the thing itself, so that one very often finds, with the works of Giotto, that people's eyes are deceived and they mistake the picture for the real thing." And Stephen, one of his most valorous pupils, was called an "aper of nature".

The concept of perspective, the acme of the Renaissance artistic revolution, stands at the intersection between the science of sight and the art of deception. What we have is an ordered and logical system of proportions that permits the portrayal in two dimensions of what our eyes see in three, a feat accomplished not because of the illusionistic talents of the individual artist but because there is a pool of shared theoretical knowledge. This is one of the fruits of the rational thought that presides over all Renaissance art, "which," we are advised by Leonardo da Vinci, "with philosophy and subtle speculation considers all the qualities of the forms", while at the same time bringing back to life the dream of a virtuosity whose aim is not to convince the intellect, but to astonish the eye. Giovanni Santi, Raphael's father, praises Andrea Mantegna in verse because "fa stupire / qualunque i scorti suoi vede e remira, / che inganan l'occhio e l'arte fan gioire" (he astounds / all those who gaze upon his vistas / which deceive the eye and exalt art).

Mantegna gives proof of his talents in the *Camera Picta*, or *Camera degli Sposi*, in the Palazzo Ducale of Mantua. It is a smallish room in which the artist uses a complex scheme of painted architectural elements opening onto landscapes to trick the eye into perceiving a much larger room culminating above in a fake oculus, opening on the sky, through which we see a number of figures. We stand awestruck as the infinite heavens open wide above us, when in fact it is all painted on a ceiling that is only slightly vaulted.

We are now in the 1460s and '70s. Almost contemporaneously, Donato Bramante is hired by Gian Galeazzo Visconti to refurbish the church of Santa Maria presso San Satiro. The space where the apse should be is inexorably blocked off by a solid wall. Bramante thus resorts to paint and relief to create a false perspective with semi-columns receding into the background and continuing the line of real columns towards a completely illusory apse, but one that succeeds in giving the altar the sort of noble spatial setting that befits it.

But it is the meeting between fifteenth-century Italian perspective and Flemish art, at the close of the century, that gave birth to what we may call bona fide trompe l'oeil, a painted image conceived and crafted to deceive the viewer.

The paintings of the Flemish artists Jan van Eyck, Joos van Gent, Hugo van der Goes, Rogier van der Weyden and Pedro Berruguete brought to Italian Renaissance art an example of a means of artistic representation that captured not only the architecture of the forms, but also—and decisively—the relationship between the forms and light through the use of colour. Hence we have a perceptive effect that the artist analyses and meticulously and minutely recreates in his or her work. This was enhanced by the new technique of oil painting prac-

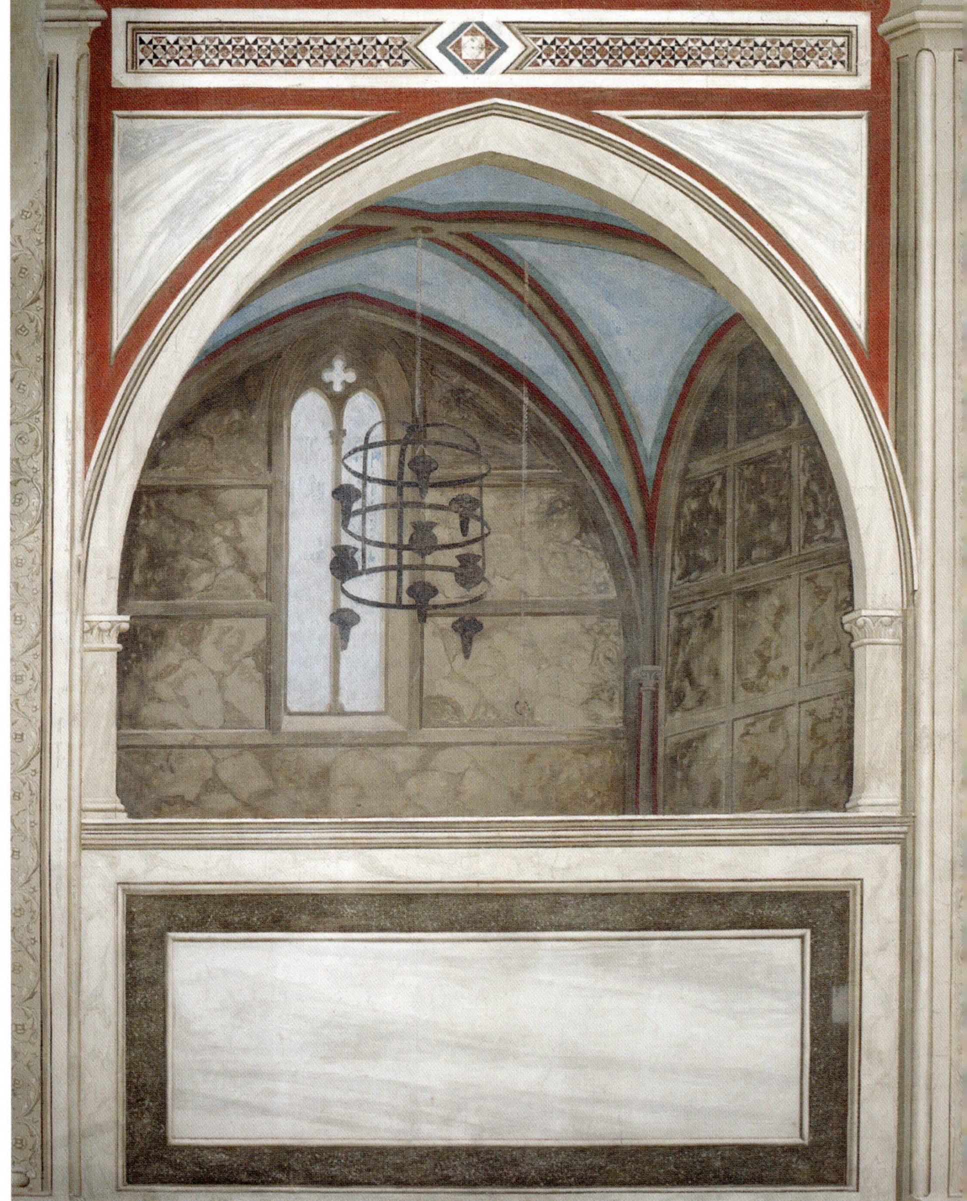

ticed by the Flemish, allowing greater faithfulness to detail and, by means of glazing (the overlaying of extremely thin layers of almost transparent colour), luminous effects of extraordinary verisimilitude.

Triumphant sixteenth-century art, from Mannerism to the Baroque, made good use of these teachings. A determining impulse came from scenography, which early on in the century witnessed the spread of scenes painted with illusions of perspective. This was seen in the productions of *Cassaria* and *I Suppositi* by Ludovico Ariosto in 1508 and 1509 at the court of the Este family in Ferrara, and in subsequent productions at the courts of Urbino, Florence and Rome that were the work of such artists as Gerolamo Genga, Baldassarre Peruzzi, Bastiano da Sangallo and Domenico Ghirlandaio. In 1545, Sebastiano Serlio penned a *Treatise on Scenes* in his *Second Book of Architecture*, with three engravings that illustrate the sophisticated use of both physical and painted illusionistic elements.

If Correggio's *The Vision of St. John the Evangelist on Patmos*, painted in 1520-21 in the church of San Giovanni Evangelista in Parma, is a painted work in which the trompe l'oeil technique already exhibits its nature as sophisticated virtuoso exhibition, but still in the service of an idea, the *Sala dei Giganti* conceived by Giulio Romano for the Palazzo Te in Mantua some ten years later (1532-35) is a perfect fusion of painting and theatre. Zeus hurls his thunderbolts at the Titans from the illusory heights of a false cupola. The Titans tumble down the walls to the floor in a crush of collapsing architecture. Here the beholders do not merely behold the scene, they find themselves a part of it, immersed in a suggestive context which originally extended onto the coloured paving stones in the

15

floor. The physical space becomes entirely pictorial, and those who find themselves within it are direct participants in the portrayed events.

The special effect gradually began to prevail. Paolo Veronese conceived courtly illusions for the Palladian Villa Barbaro in Maser. Baroque illusions, where architectural space expands and multiplies into pure spectacle, were created by Francesco Borromini, while Pietro da Cortona executed pictorial ones at the Palazzo Barberini in Rome. When, in 1685, Andrea Pozzo painted the whirling ceiling of the Church of Sant'Ignazio in Rome, the triumph of the Baroque reached its culmination, and the eighteenth century, the time of Tiepolo and Rococo, would only extrapolate the lesson to its utmost degree.

This artistic current, inspired by scenography and dedicated to the grandiose qualities of spatial deception, was joined by another that was no less suggestive and fertile. In 1472, Federico da Montefeltro commissioned the decorations of his tiny studio in his palace in Urbino to an artist who has remained anonymous. However, for the virtuosity of his trompe l'oeil, there are many who suspect Bramante as the author. The inlaid wood panelling is a triumph of visual illusions. We see a chair with musical instruments, books and other objects; an armoire marked out with pilaster strips and half-open grillwork doors revealing codices, books, clocks, sheet music, an hourglass, a prism-shaped ink pot, and other objects; a window with a basket of fruit and a squirrel; arches opening onto a landscape; a closet with armour; statues in niches. It is all an illusion that both evokes and outdoes the lesson of the great Pompeian paintings, which had not yet been discovered at the time.

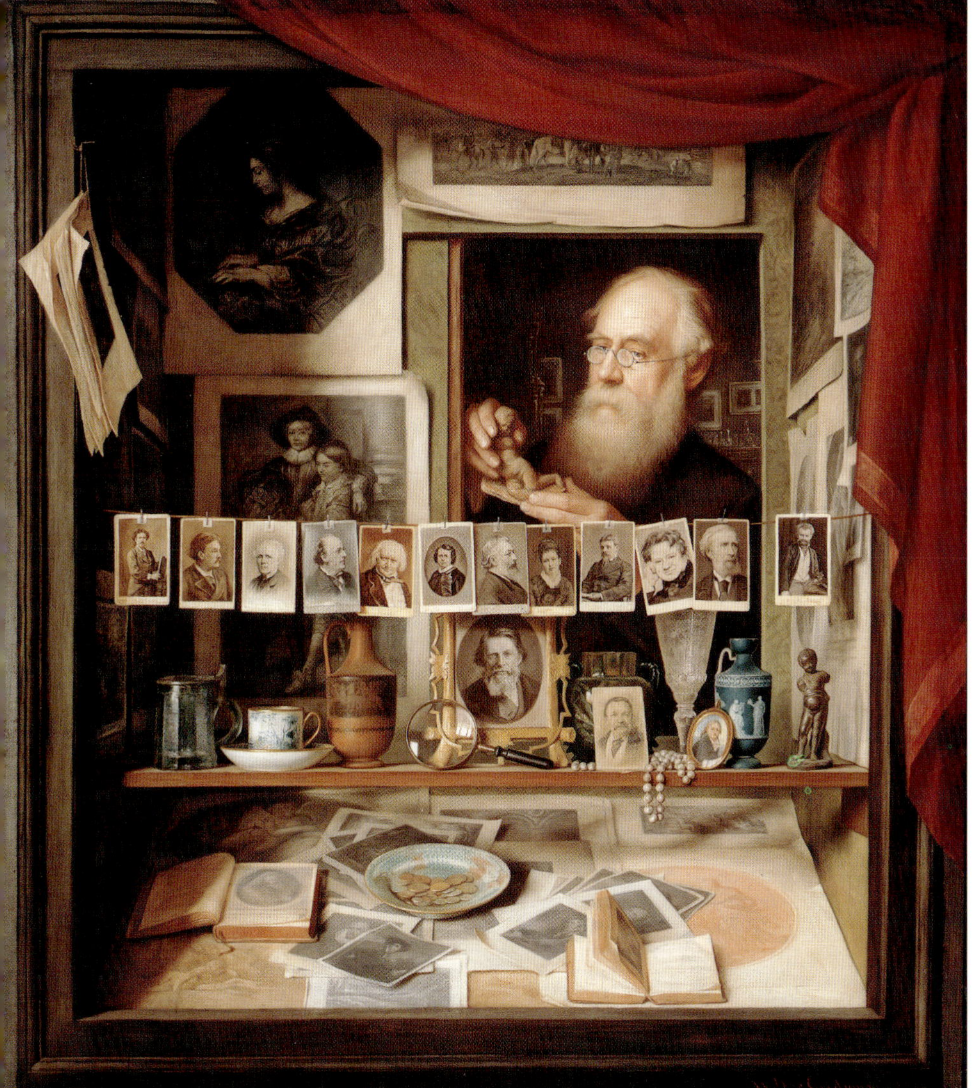

No less rich are the related inlay works which, again per order of Federico, Francesco di Giorgio hired Giuliano da Majano to do in the Palazzo Ducale of Gubbio in 1479-82. These works are now found in the New York Metropolitan Museum of Art.

These were the first utterances of the new art—or the renewed art, given its Greek and Roman precedents—of the still-life, a realm in which the trompe l'oeil technique reached some of its highest pinnacles. Vasari reminds us that Giovanni da Udine, one of Raphael's pupils and collaborators, "did a fine job of counterfeiting... all natural things, animals, drapes, instruments, vases, towns, houses and greenery". And in the early years of the seventeenth century, Vincenzo Giustiniani—one of the most prestigious patrons of Caravaggio, whose *Basket of Fruit* is one of the great masterpieces of the late sixteenth century—describes in a letter the spread "not just in Rome, in Venice and other parts of Italy, but also in Flanders and in France" of the fashion of a kind of easel painting, whose motif was "the able depiction of flowers and other tiny things", also noting that "Caravaggio said that it is just as difficult to make a good painting of flowers as it is to create one with figures". Hence, these works could rightfully take their place among their counterparts in terms of effort, ability and dignity.

In a few years, compositions with flowers, fruits, musical instruments, books, weapons, exotic curios and other inanimate objects became a part of aristocratic collections, alongside devotional or mythological paintings, and meriting equal respect. Their strength lay in the charm of their often mimetic reproduction of the real, in the illusionistic virtuosity achieved by the artist. In Italy these subjects were called *oggetti di ferma* (still objects); in the Netherlands, where the old Flemish tradition produced true geniuses in the genre, they became known as *Still-leven*, whence the

German *Still-leben* and the English Still-life, indicating that the model is immobile nature rather than something alive and dynamic. The eighteenth-century French expression *nature morte* was originally a negative term, but from it derives the current Italian term *natura morta*.

Flowers and fruit were soon joined by foods, such as fish and game for both decorative and scientific purposes. One example is the eighteen volumes of faithful descriptive plates of the "theatre of nature" commissioned in Bologna by the scientist Ulisse Aldrovandi, and Jacopo Ligozzi's minutely detailed floral works for the Florentine court.

Primacy in still-lifes was achieved in Flanders and in Holland, with masters such as Frans Snyders and Jan Fyt, Pieter Claeszoon and Willem Claeszoon Heda, Willem Kalf and Willem van Aelst, Osias Beert and Abraham van Beyeren, Maerten Boelema de Stomme and the Bosschaerts, the Brueghels, and Floris Claeszoon van Dijck, Juan van der Hamen and Willem Kalf, Jan de Heem and Floris van Schooten, whose paintings and painting styles became known throughout Europe.

But Spain also had her masters in Juan Sanchez Cotán and Francisco de Zurbarán, Juan de Arellano and Francisco Barrera, Pedro Camprobín and Juan de Espinosa; France hers with Lubin Baugin and Alexandre-François Desportes, Louise Moillon and Sébastien Stoskopff, Jean-Baptiste-Siméon Chardin and Jean-Baptiste Oudry; and Italy with Fede Galizia and Evaristo Baschenis, Paolo Porpora and Giuseppe Recco, Giovan Battista Ruoppolo and Margherita Caffi, Bartolomeo Bimbi and Giovanna Garzoni, Bernardo Strozzi and Felice Boselli. The practice of the still-life thus became quite widespread, and a maniacal faithfulness to the subject became a factor of quality.

In this array of masters, some stand out for a bona fide specialisation in trompe l'oeil. One example is Cornelius Norbertus Gijsbrechts, Flemish, working in the second half of the seventeenth century. He created paintings whose main purpose was to offer strange and deceptive views. His most famous work shows the back side of a painting with its frame, nails and inventory tag in a sophisticated conceptual game. Gijsbrechts' contemporary, Samuel van Hoogstraten, created a number of similar works, as did Giuseppe Maria Crespi, who painted his famous *Bookcase* with shelves, books and writing implements in 1725.

While trompe l'oeil is a product characteristic of the Mannerist and Baroque culture, and while its main substance is an ability to deceive the eye via manual artifice, the utopian dream of a perfect representation of the visible took other roads, associated with the study of the laws of optics and vision.

Writings existed in the Middle Ages on the *camera obscura*, a stenopaic apparatus that captured faithful images. Arab scientists such as Al-Kindi and Al-Hazen left fundamental treatises translated in Europe, inspiring numerous scientific experiments in precise perspectives involving figures such as Leon Battista Alberti, Leonardo da Vinci, and Albrecht Dürer. In the mid seventeenth century, the erudite Athanasius Kircher described a gigantic camera obscura with an optical lens, large enough to contain its designer. This was the ancestor both of the camera and of the "magic lantern", a rudimental but fascinating precursor to the cinema.

The eighteenth-century landscape painters, with Canaletto and Bernardo Bellotto first and foremost, made broad use of this instrument to obtain large-scale images with perfect perspective and fine

Andrea Mantegna
*Oculus in the ceiling
of the* Camera degli Sposi,
1467-74
Fresco
Palazzo Ducale, Mantua

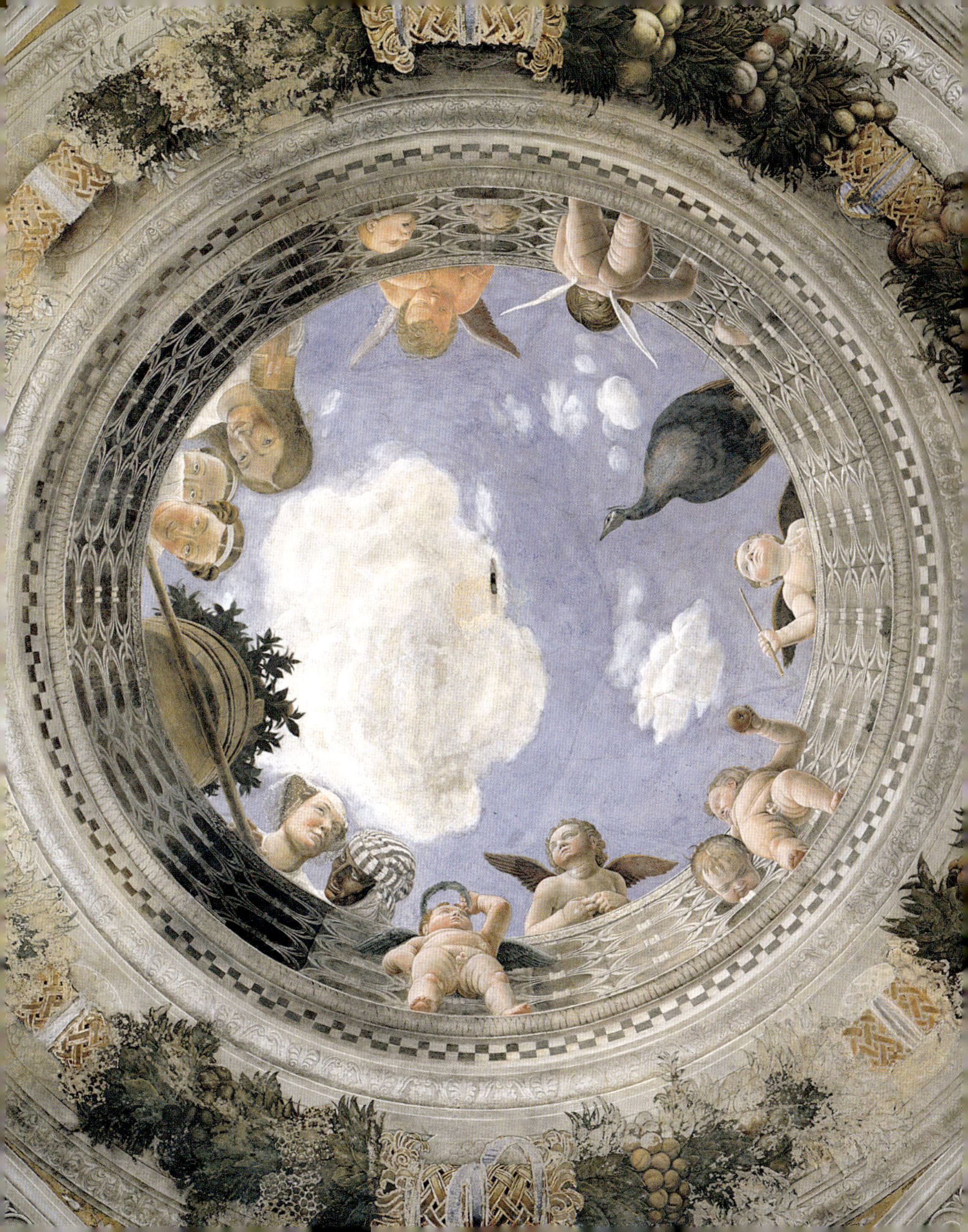

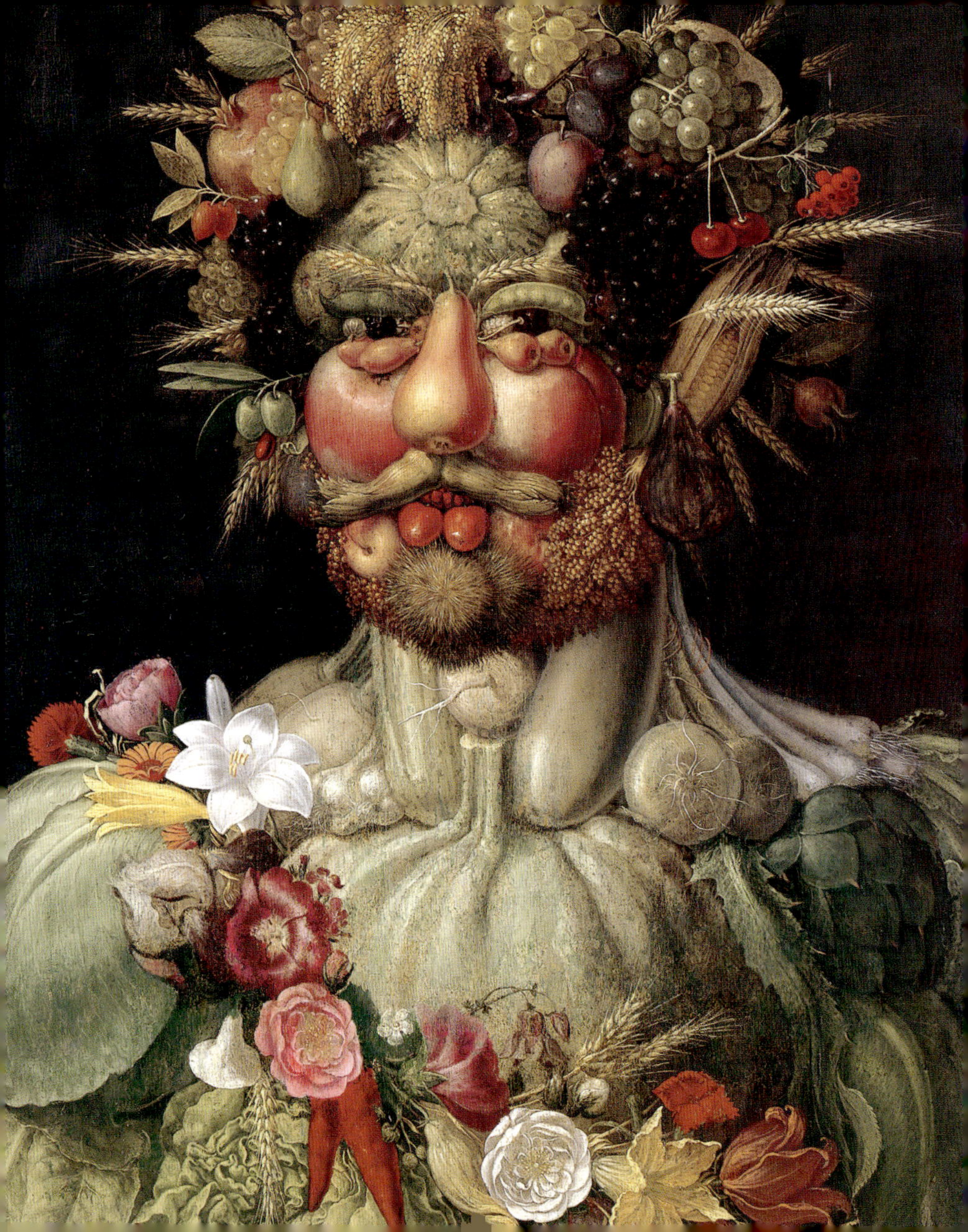

detail. And it was the camera obscura that gave Joseph Nicéphore Niépce and Louis Daguerre their start in creating the earliest photographs in the 1820s. It is noteworthy to recall that Daguerre was a scenographer, and that in 1822 he opened the Diorama in Paris. The diorama was a show with scenes painted on a series of translucent linen panels arranged in a sort of truncated tunnel. Depending on how they were lighted, the scenes appeared to change in an illusory way that prompted amazement and even fright among the audience.

It is true that when photography first appeared, it was considered to be the agent of the inevitable demise of painting, as we read in the critical essay by Baudelaire cited above. However, it is equally true that photography was not considered to be illusionistic enough to satisfy the desire for wonder that was now widely sought by audiences. For this reason, the introduction of the stereoscope by the physicist David Brewster at the 1851 London World's Fair caused a much greater stir than had the emergence of photography. The stereoscope was an instrument based on the principles of binocular vision that allowed people to see three-dimensional images by presenting a slightly different image to each eye, mimicking the way our eyes see the same object from slightly different perspectives.

Its success was enormous. Between 1854 and 1856, the London Stereoscopic Company sold somewhere in the neighbourhood of half a million stereoscopes and had a catalogue of one hundred thousand images. Baudelaire, highly critical of the new myth of illusionistically perfect views, was back on the attack, noting that "it was not long before thousands of pairs of greedy eyes were glued to the peepholes of the stereoscope as though they were the attic-windows of the infinite."

23

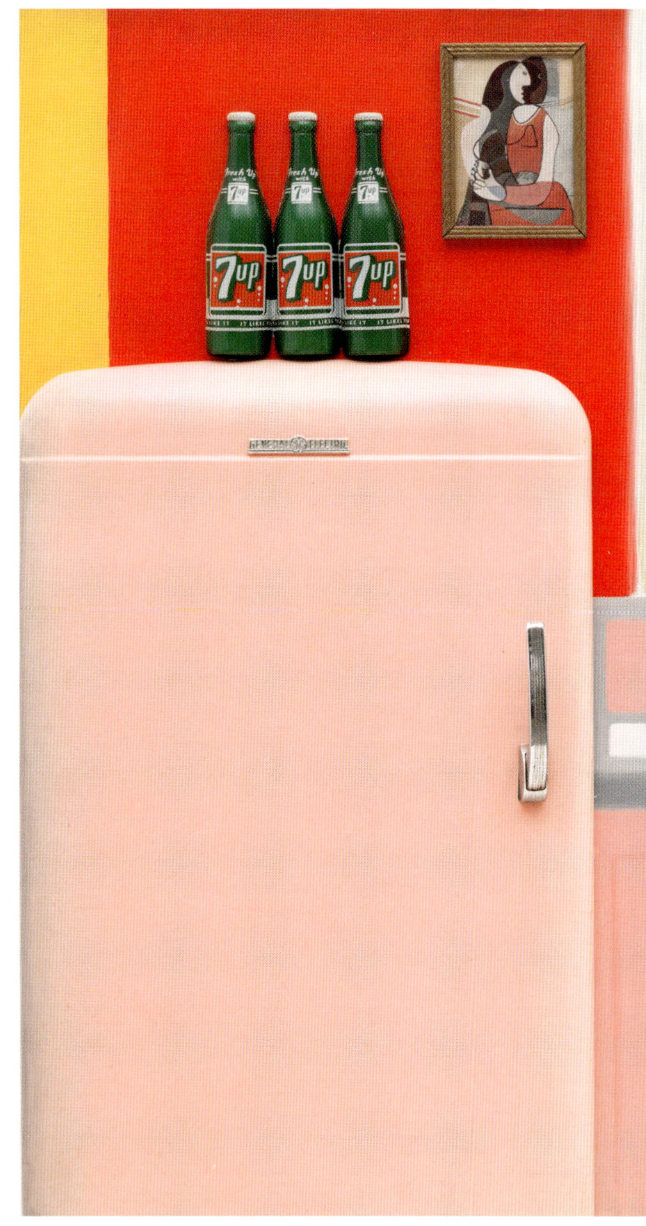

Tom Wesselmann
Still-Life #30, 1963
Oil, enamel and synthetic
polymer paint on composition
board with collage of printed
advertisements, plastic
flowers, refrigerator door,
plastic replicas of 7-Up
bottles, glazed and framed
color reproduction, and
stamped metal,
122 x 167.5 x 10 cm
The Museum of Modern Art,
New York, Gift of Philip
Johnson

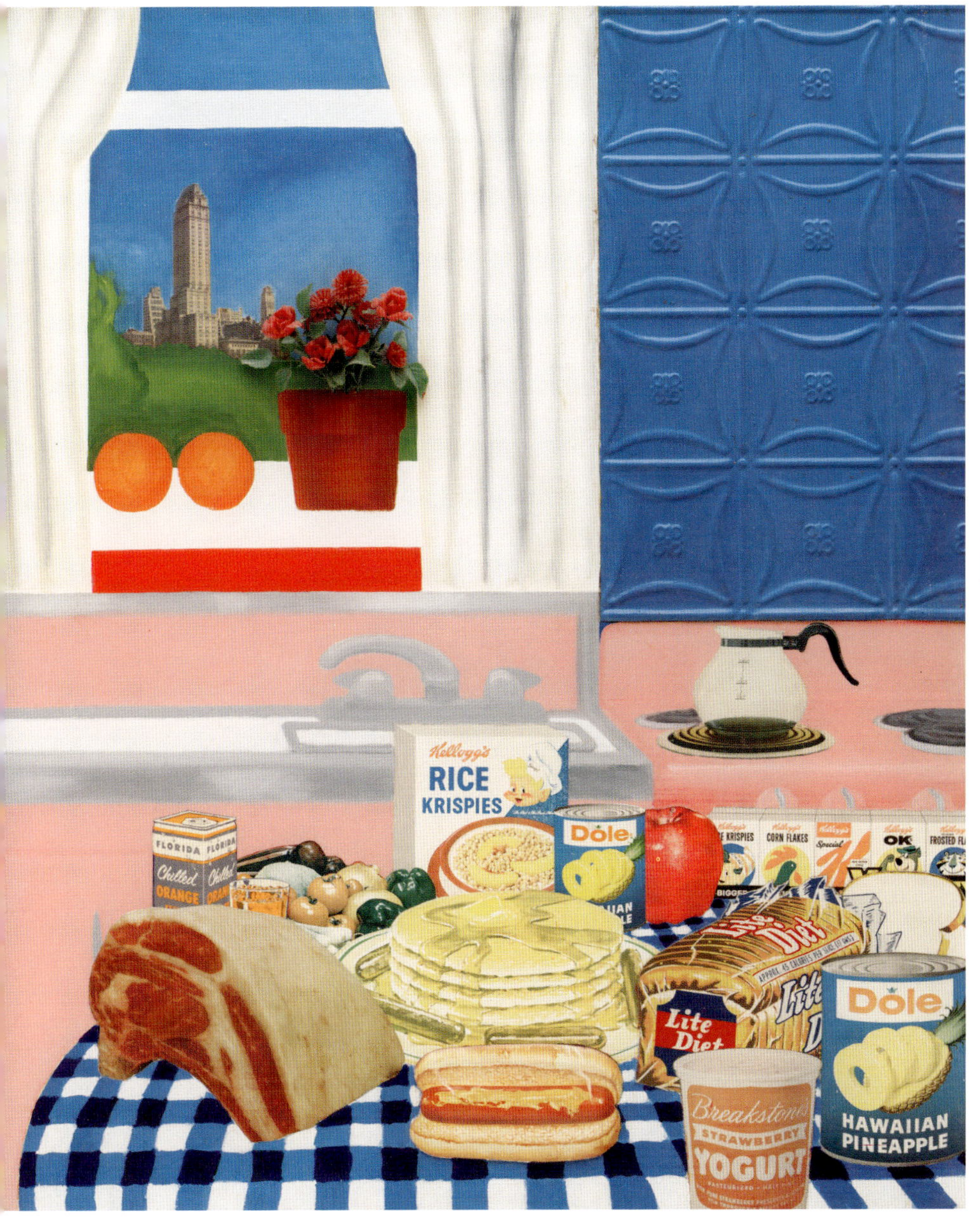
Kellogg's
RICE
KRISPIES
Dole
FLORIDA
Chilled
ORANGE
Kellogg's
CORN FLAKES
Kellogg's
Special
OK
Kellogg's
FROSTED FLAKES
Lite Diet
Lite
Diet
Breakstone's
STRAWBERRY
YOGURT
Dole
HAWAIIAN
PINEAPPLE

But the route was already laid out. In 1895, Auguste and Louis Lumière made their public presentation of their first experiments in cinema, making obsolete in a single stroke both the diorama and the stereoscope. The illusion of reality, amplified by movement, was so strong that in 1896, when they showed their *Arrivée d'un train en gare de La Ciotat*, a journalist reported that the film "had a particularly lasting impact; yes, it caused fear, terror, even panic."

From that moment on, the road of trompe l'oeil, of illusions as a vehicle for amazement and wonder, and that of the arts each when their own way.

Maurits Cornelis Escher, a fertile genius of impossible perspectives and perceptual ambiguity, is considered by many to be more a scholar than an artist. And there is a great deal of puzzlement surrounding the effective aesthetic value of works such as those of the hyperrealist artists of the 1970s, from Richard Estes to Duane Hanson, and from John De Andrea to Ralph Goings. Instead, it has been in areas such as technology and its applications to the mass consumption of images that the legacy of trompe l'oeil continues to live and breathe, from special effects at the cinema to the virtual reality created by information science.

Derrick De Kerckhove, a keen scholar of recent image consumption phenomena, writes that in the early days of trompe l'oeil, people felt a thrill akin to what we feel today with our virtual reality. It was a form of aesthetic perception that emerged in a moment of significant historical changes. Today we live in the Neo-Baroque, which, like the Baroque, is a moment of great sensory and historical change.

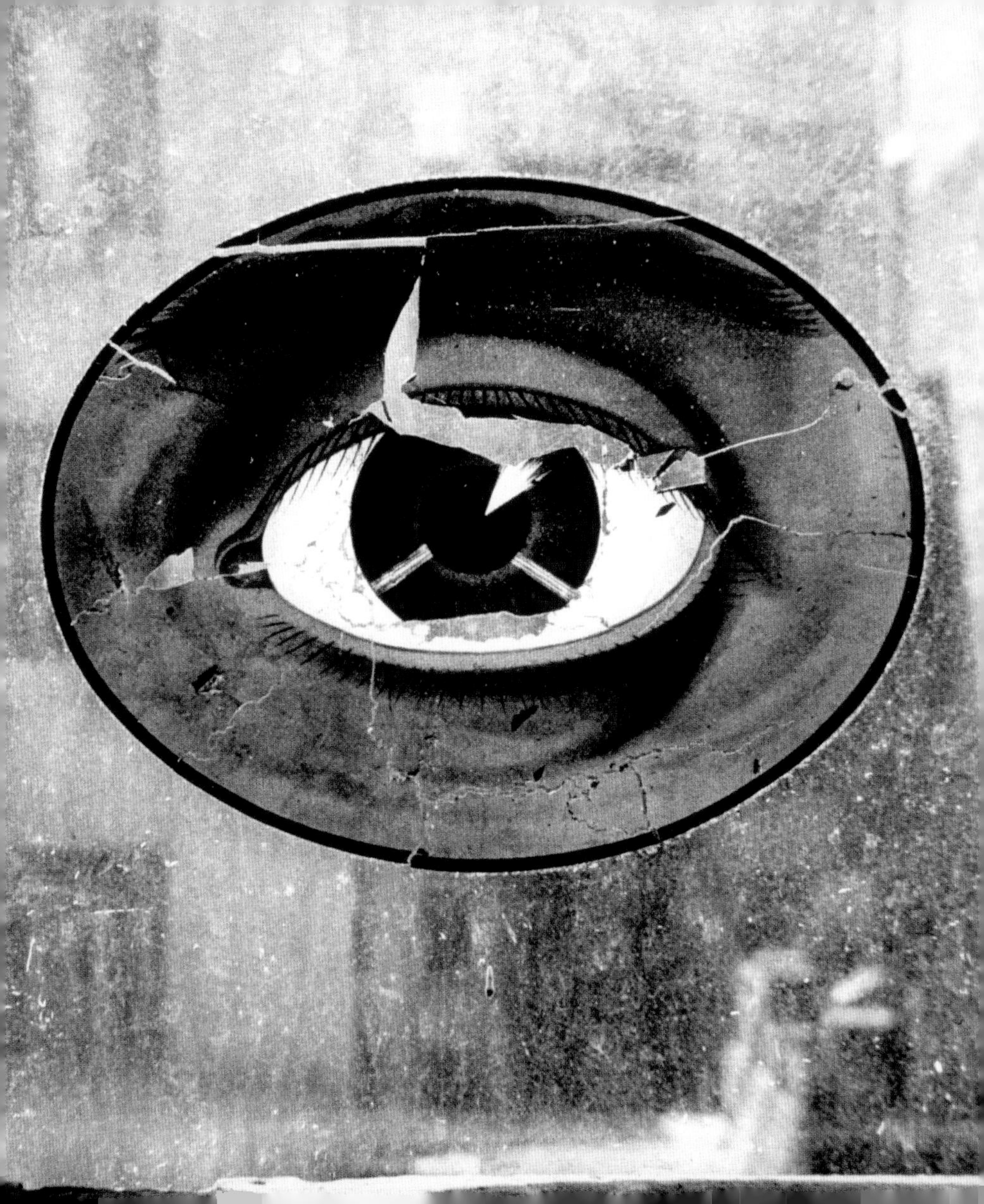

Works

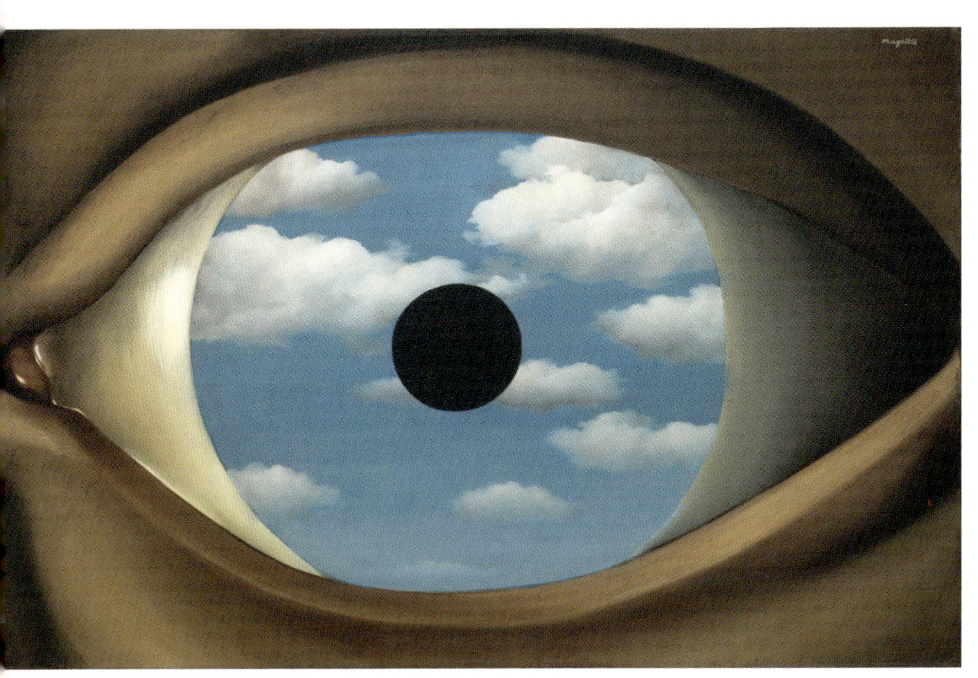

1. René Magritte
Le Faux Miroir
(*The False Mirror*), 1929

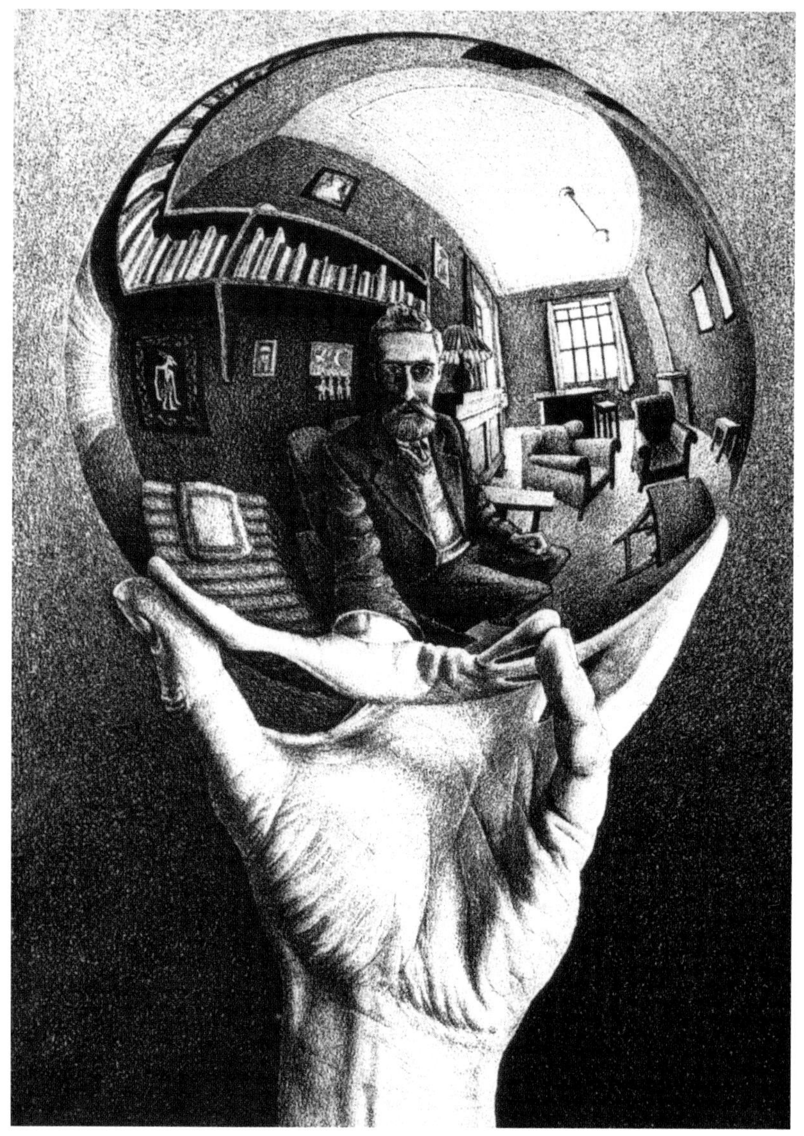

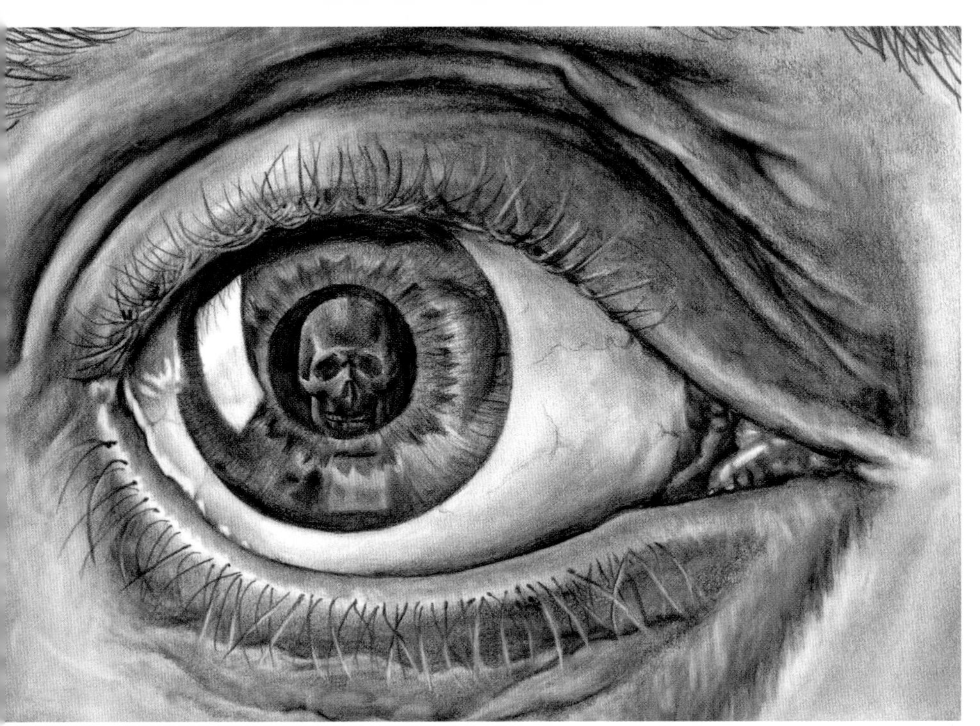

2. Maurits Cornelis Escher
Hand met spiegelende bol
(*Hand with reflecting globe*)
(detail), 1935

3. Maurits Cornelis Escher
Eye, 1946

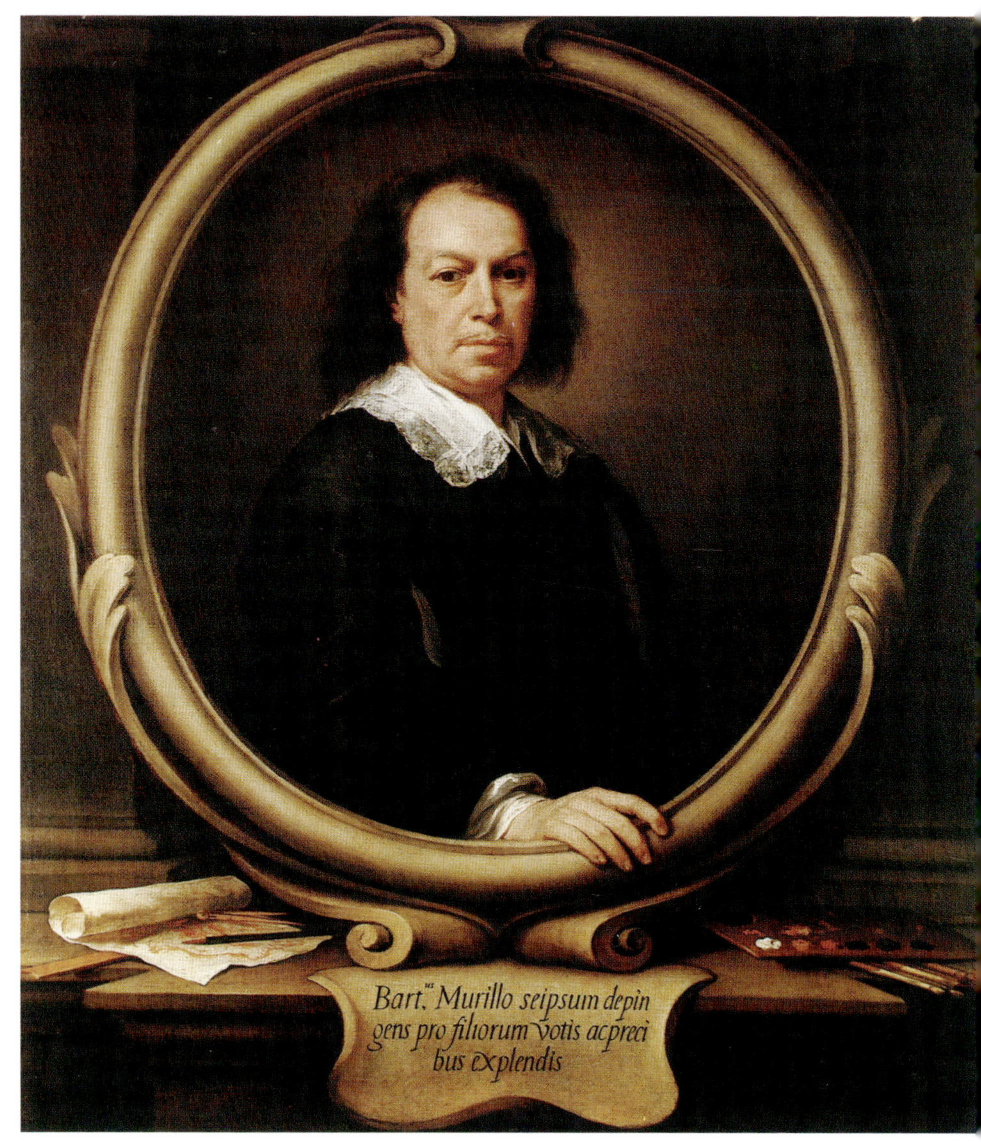

Bart.ᵘˢ Murillo seipsum depin
gens pro filiorum votis acpreci
bus explendis

32

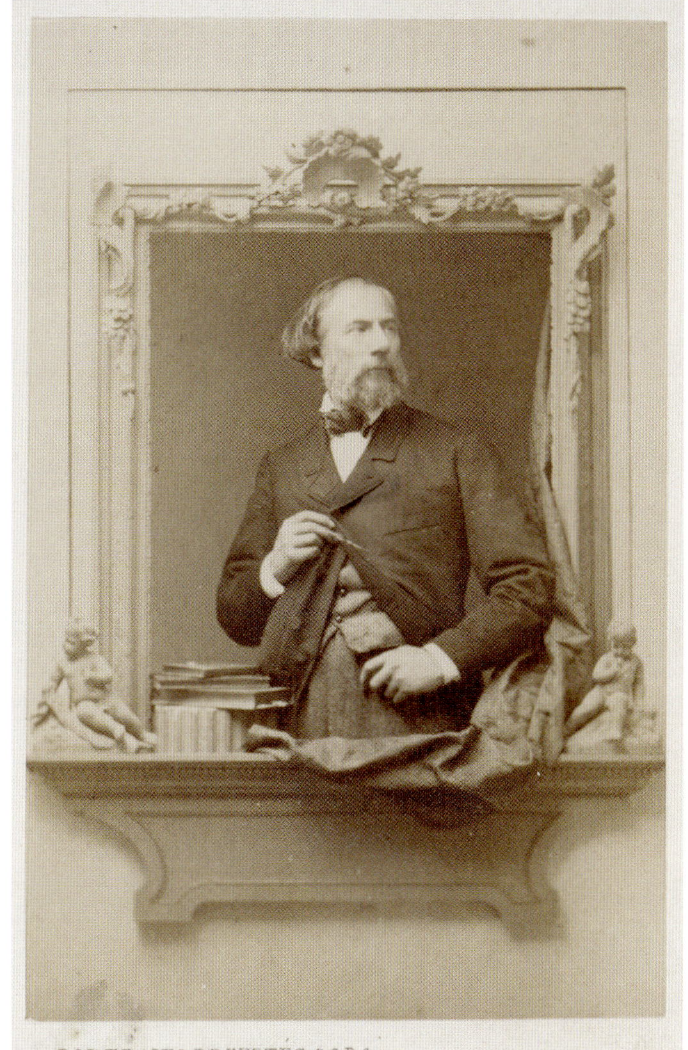

4. Bartolomé Esteban Murillo
Self-Portrait, 1670-75

5. Adolphe-Jean-François Dallemagne
Unidentified Painter, 1866

33

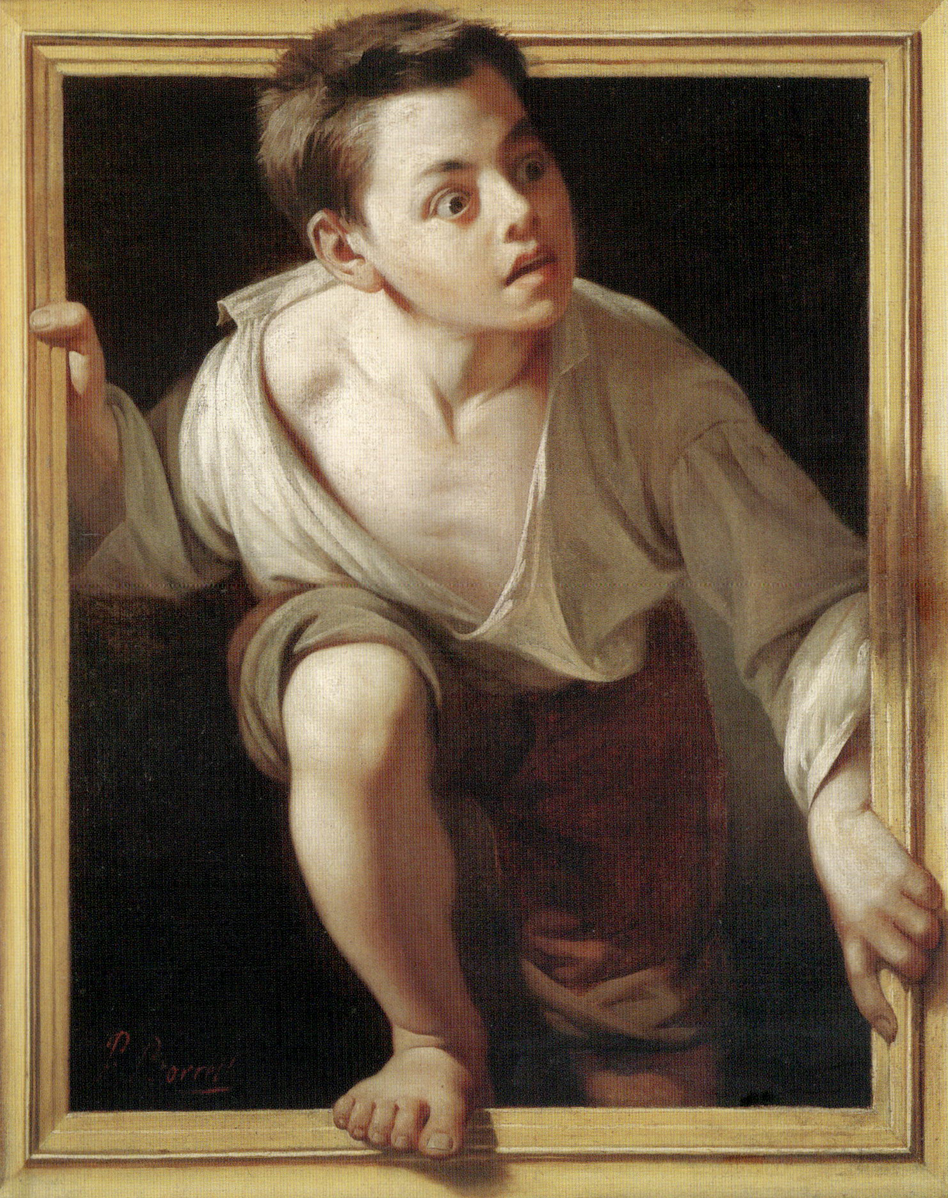

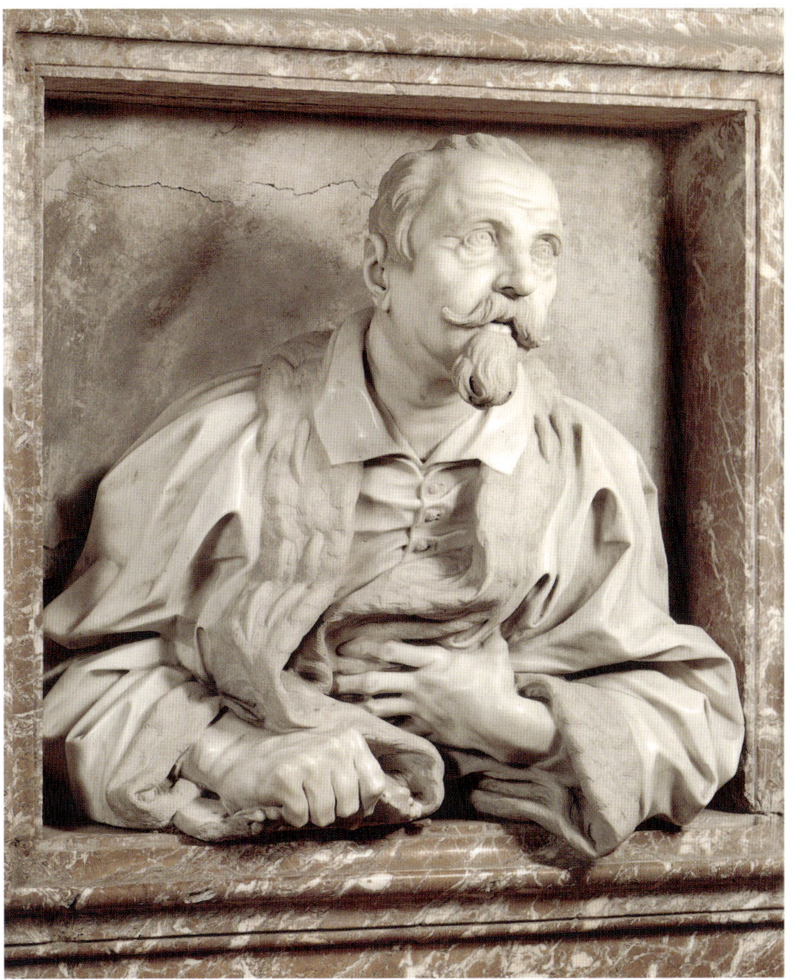

6. Pere Borrell del Caso
Escapando de la critica
(*Fleeing the critics*), 1874

7. Gian Lorenzo Bernini
Bust of Gabriele Fonseca,
1663-70

Following pages

8. Gian Lorenzo Bernini
Cardinals from the Cornaro
family, 1647-52

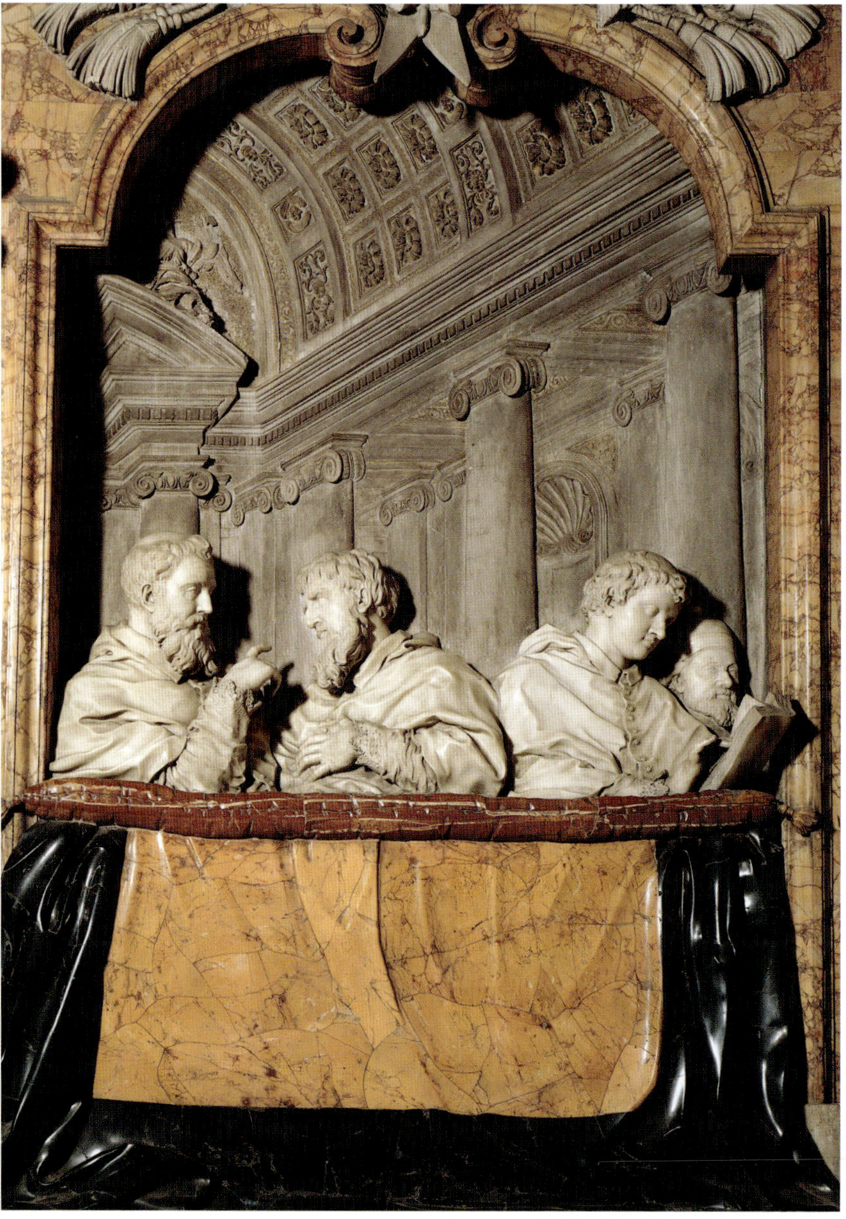

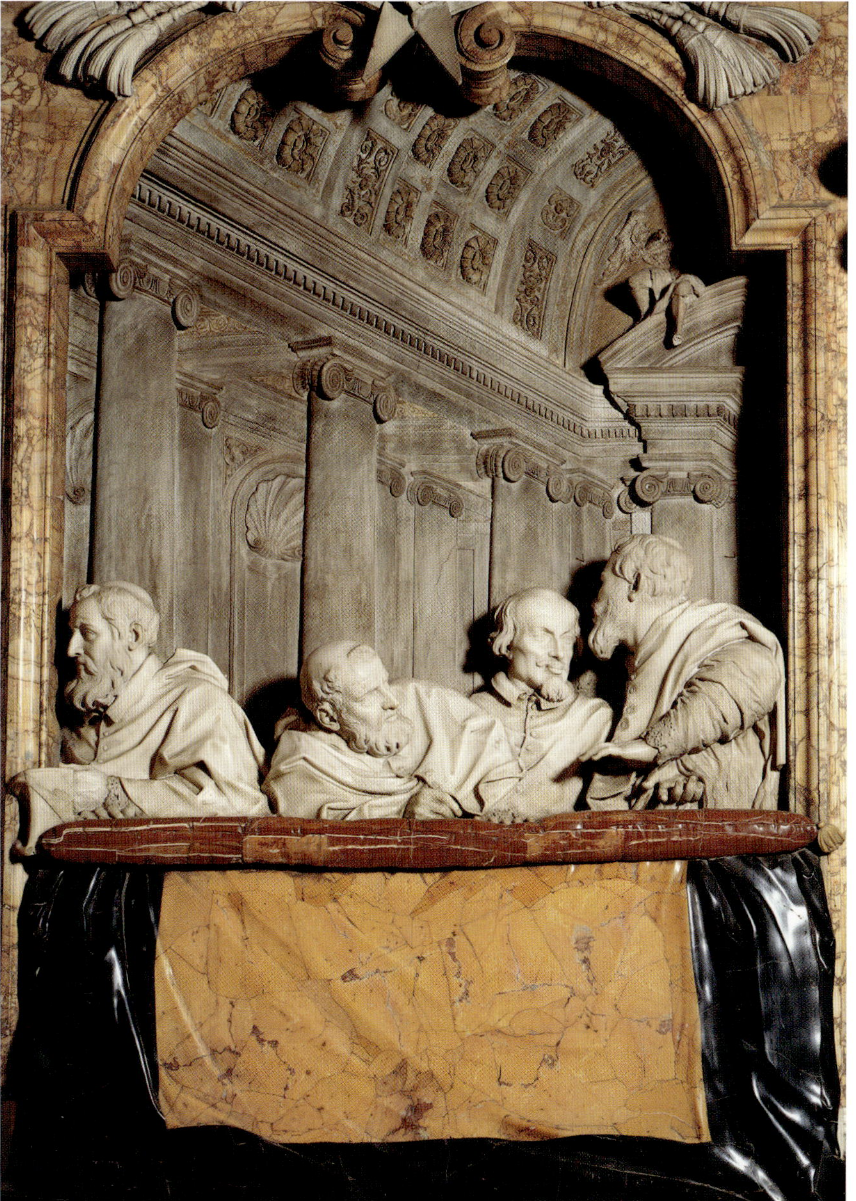

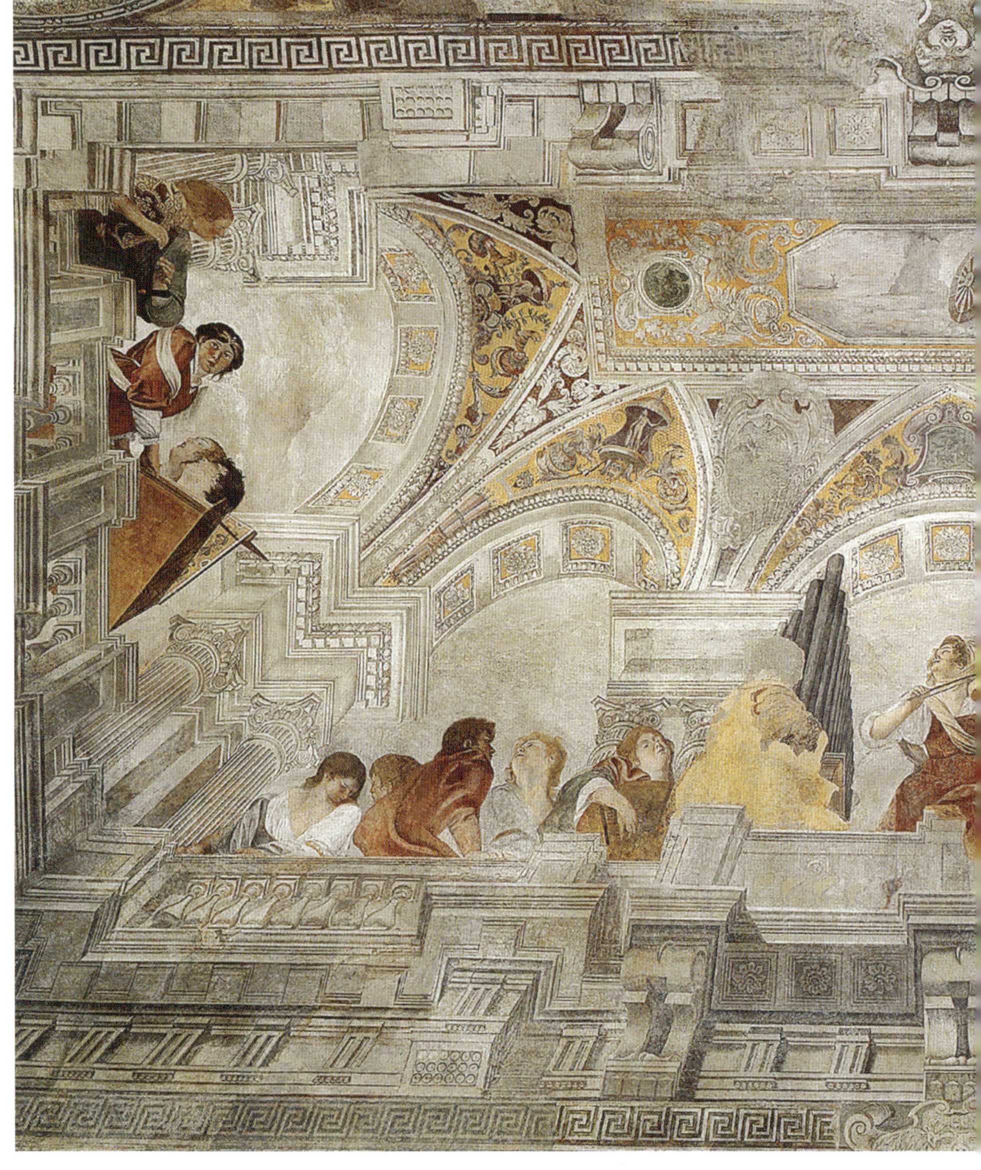

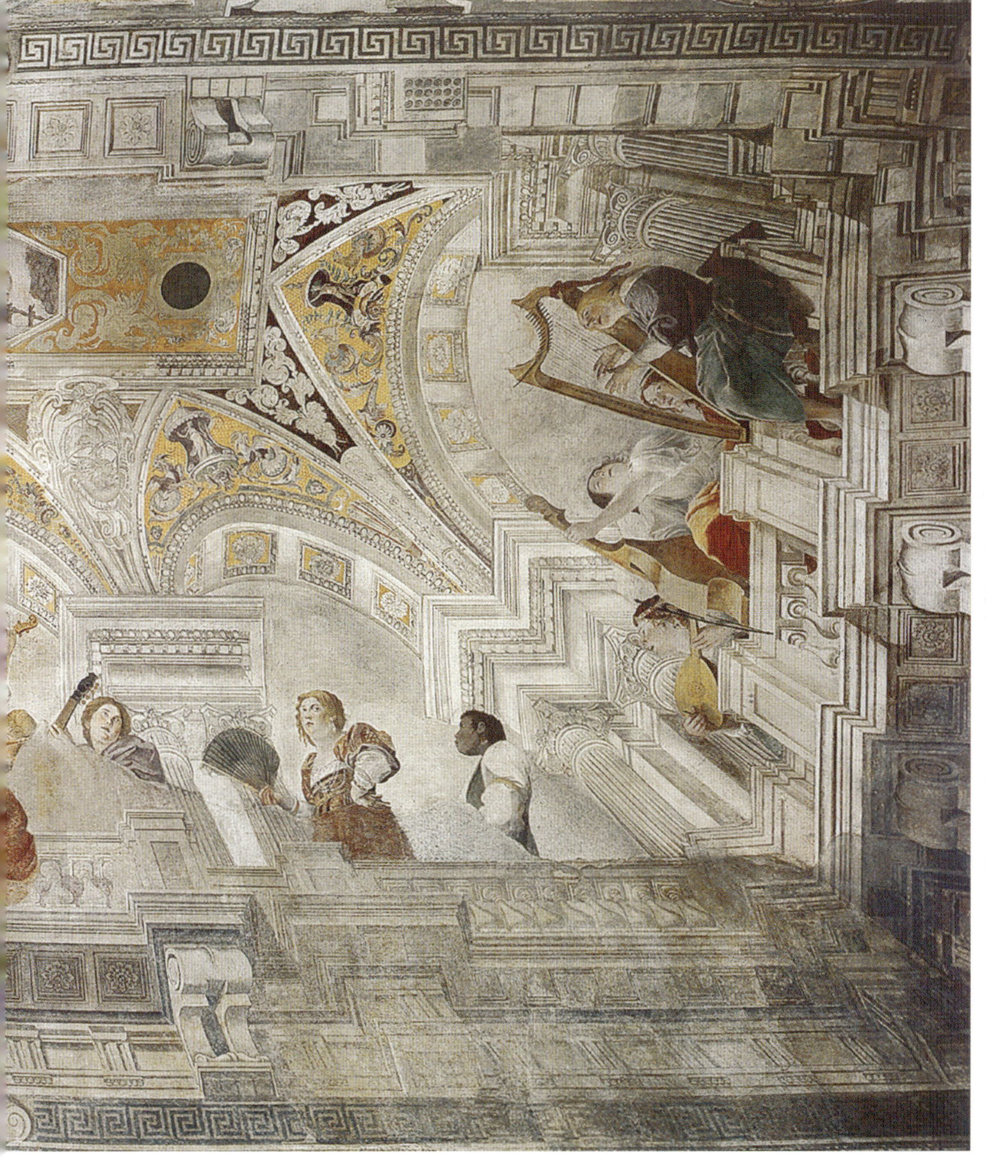

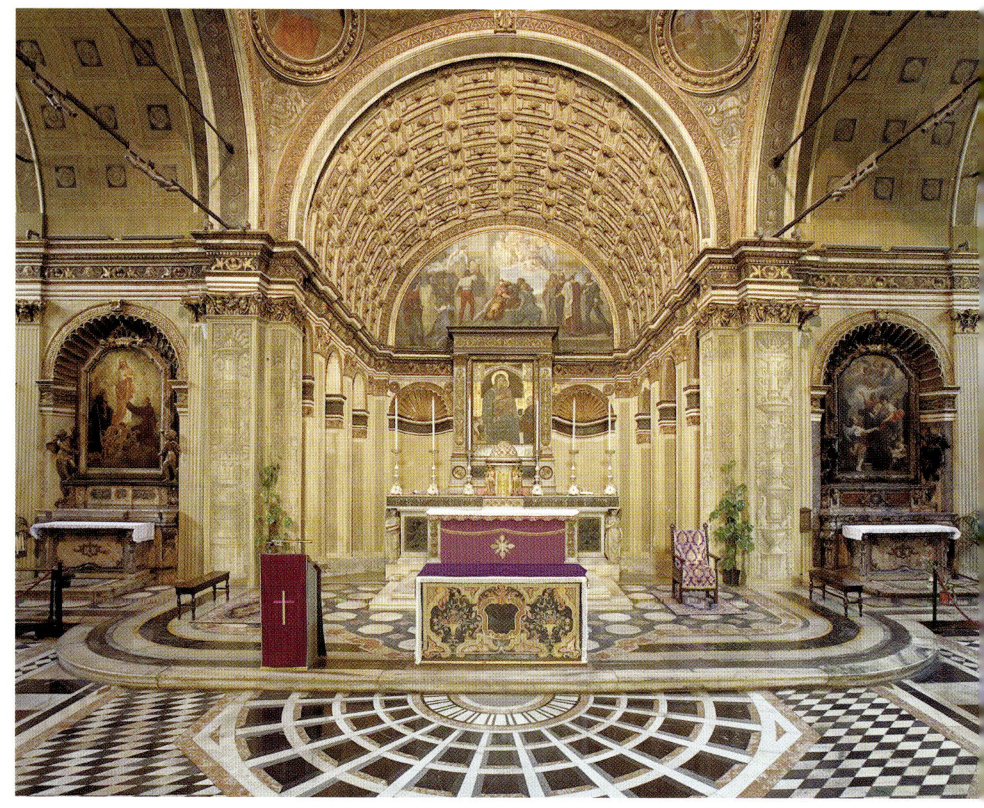

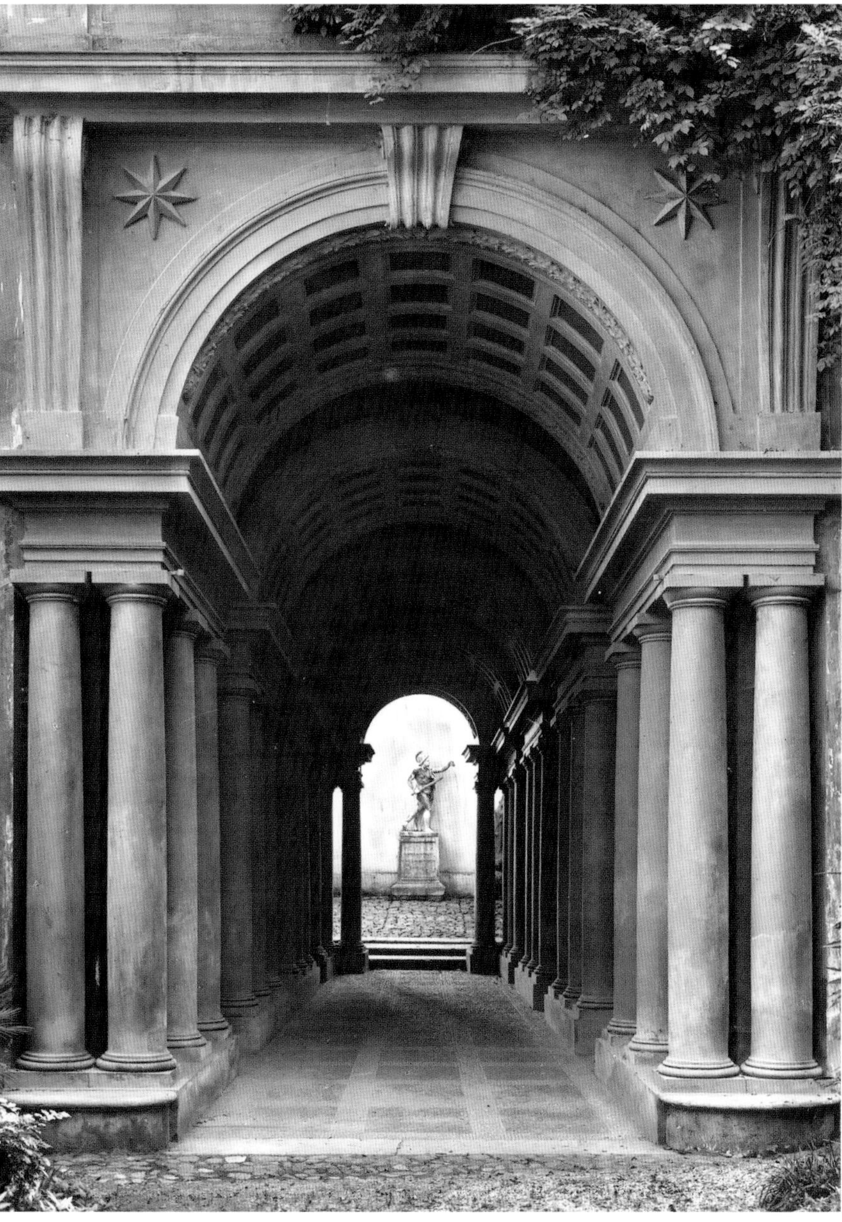

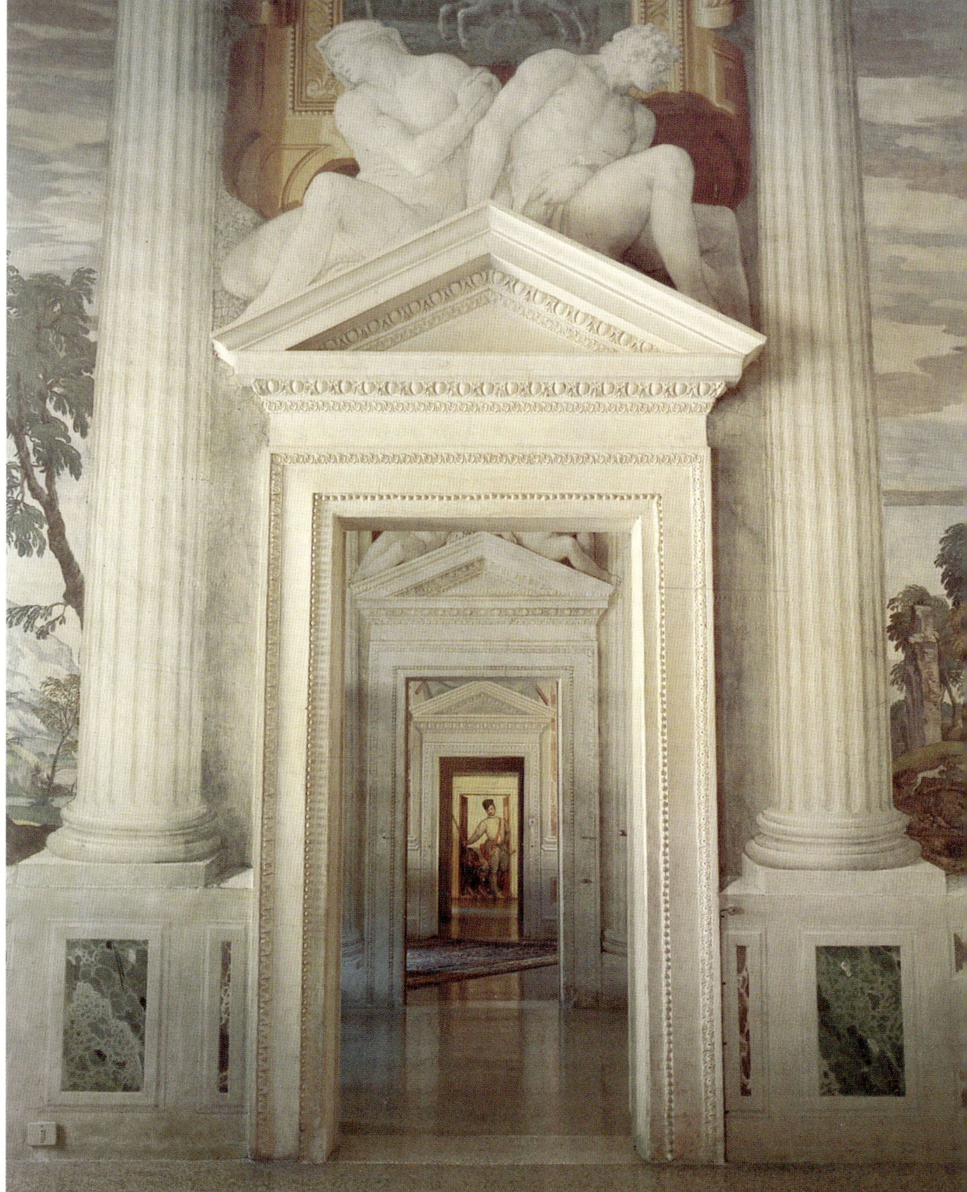

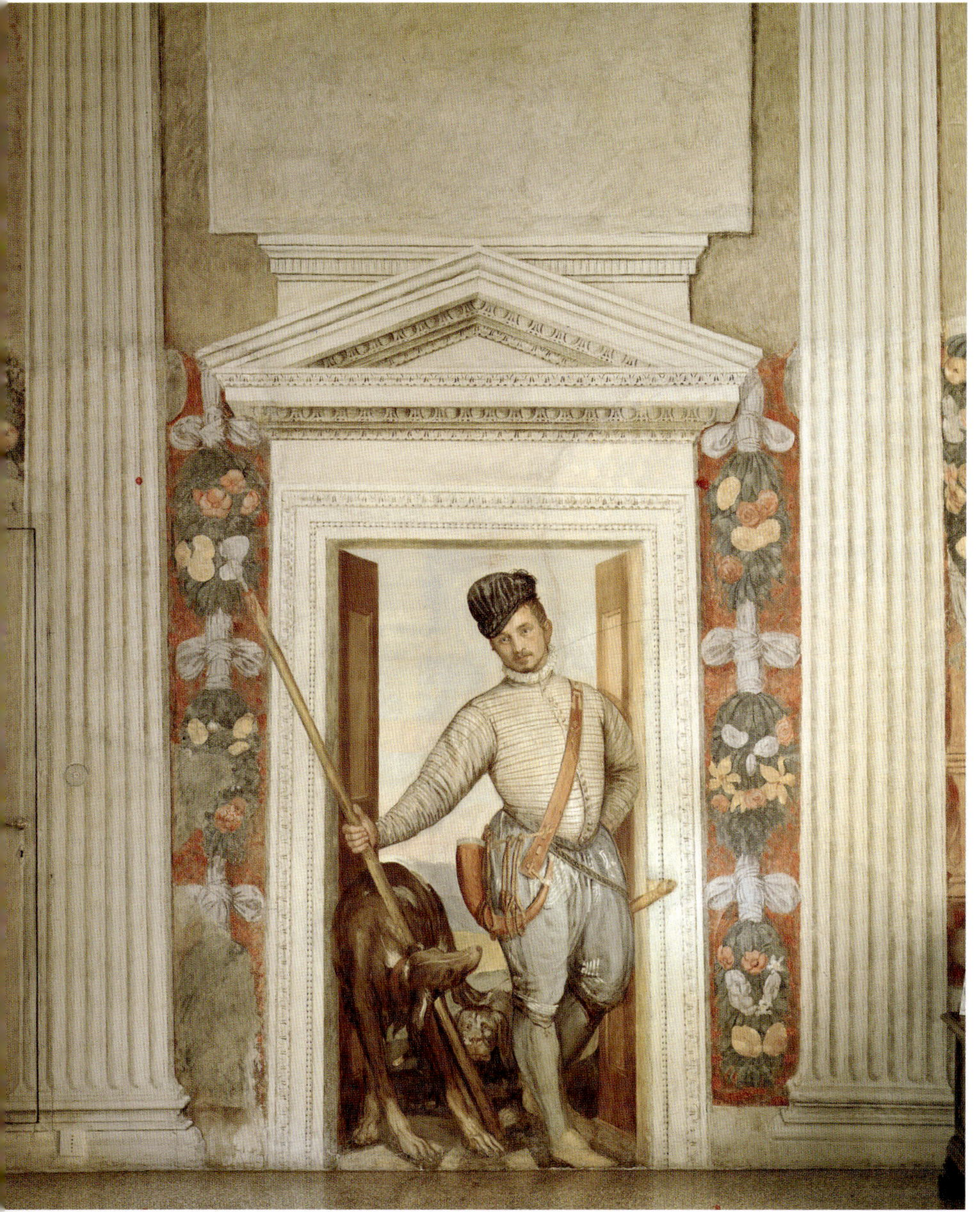

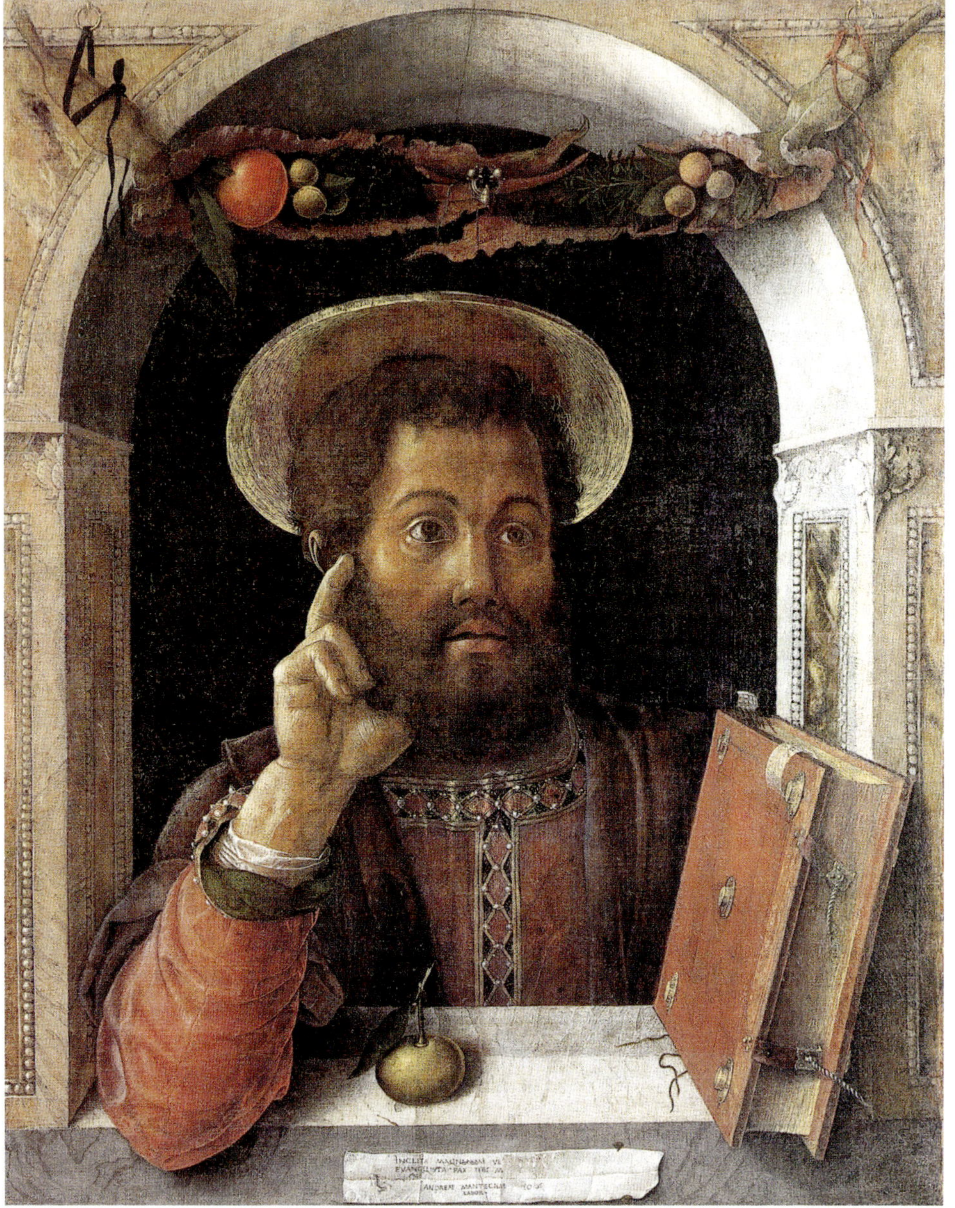
INCLITA MANTUANEM VE
EVANGELISTA · PAX TIBI M.
ANDREAE MANTEGNAE
LABOR

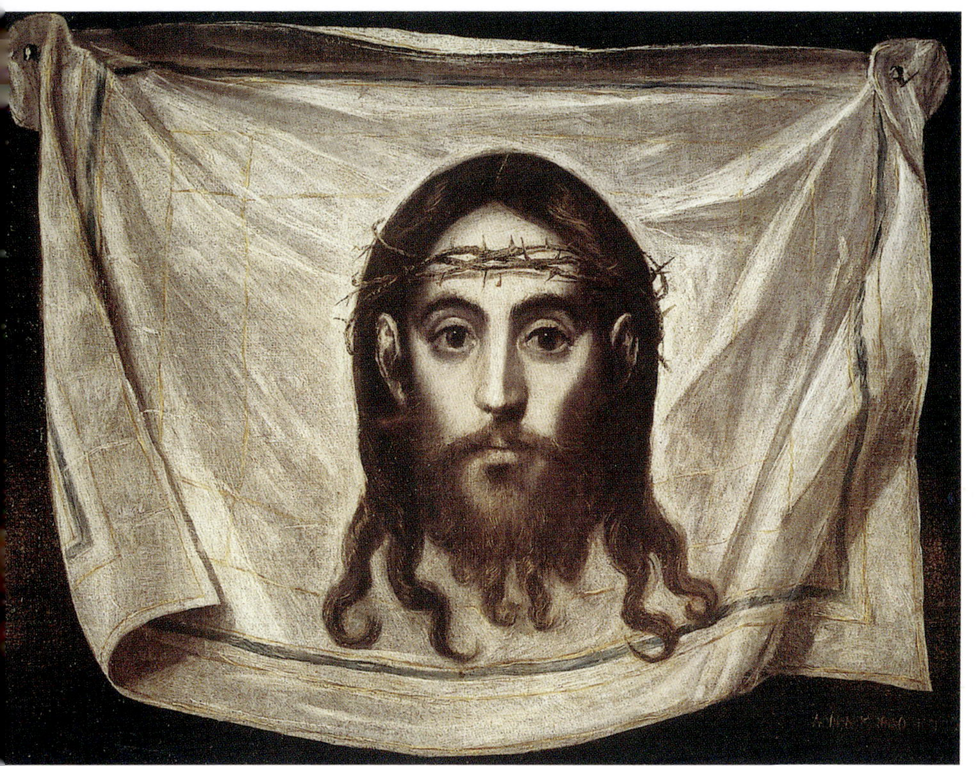

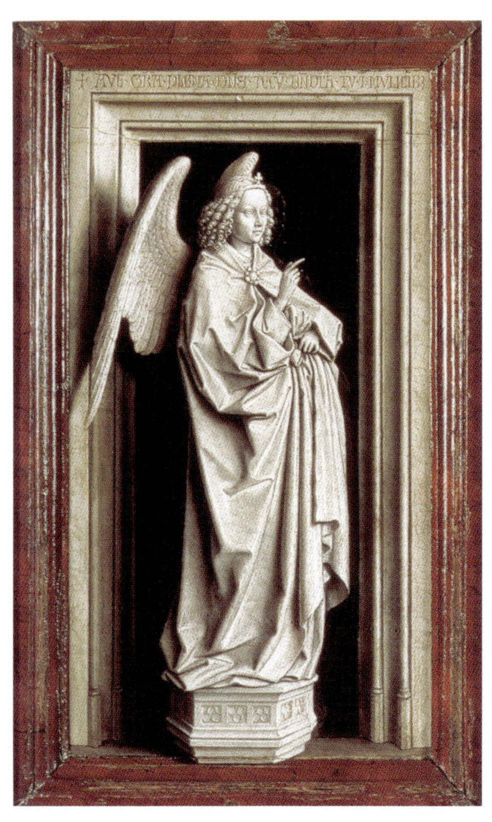

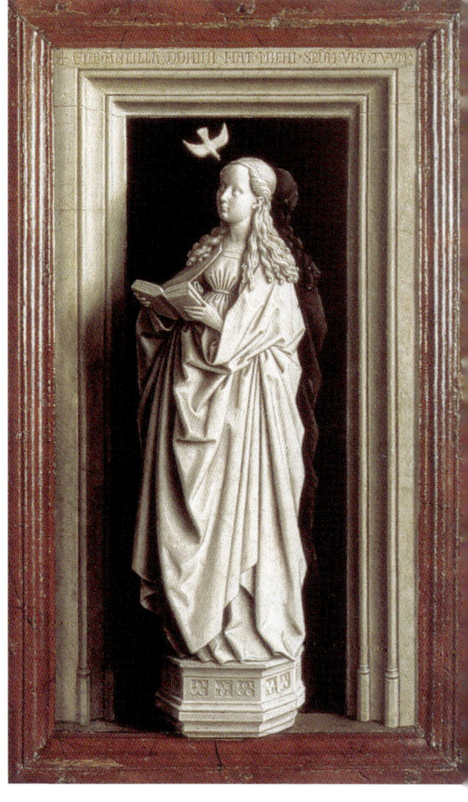

16 a, b. Jan van Eyck
Annunciation, circa 1435

17. Roger van der Weyden
Madonna with Child
(*Madonna Durán*), 1435-40

Following pages
18. Jean-Marie Faverjon
Trompe l'oeil Self-Portrait,
circa 1868

**19. Jean-Baptiste
Perroneau**
Portrait of Jean-Baptiste
Oudry, 1753

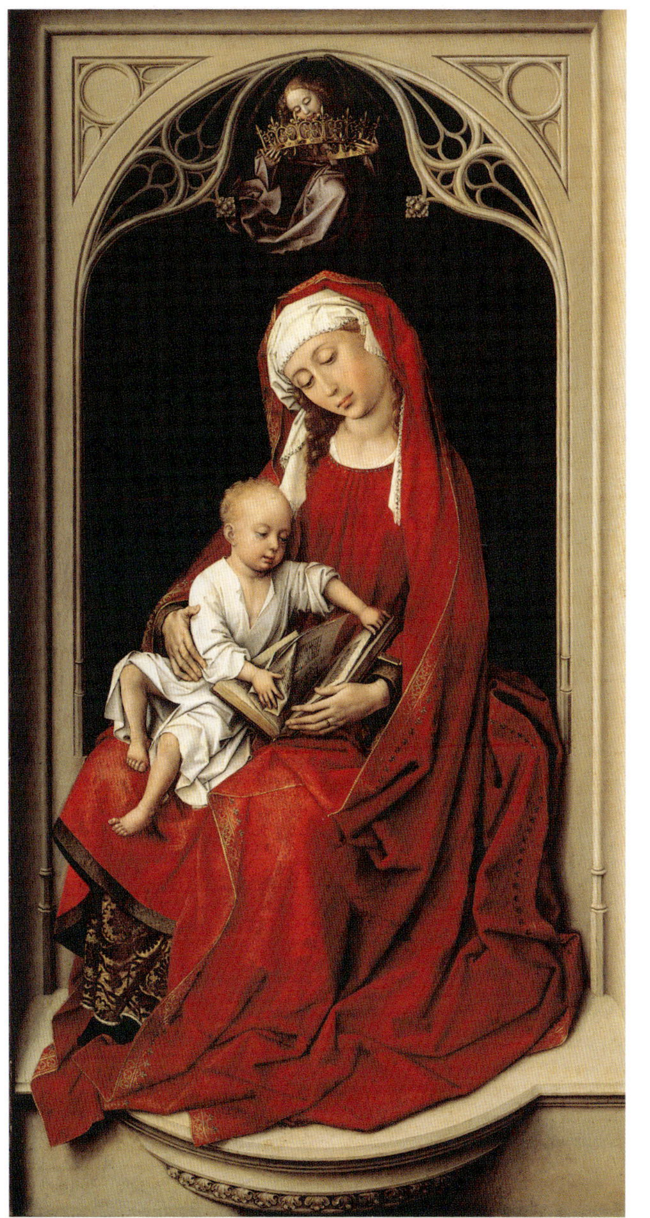

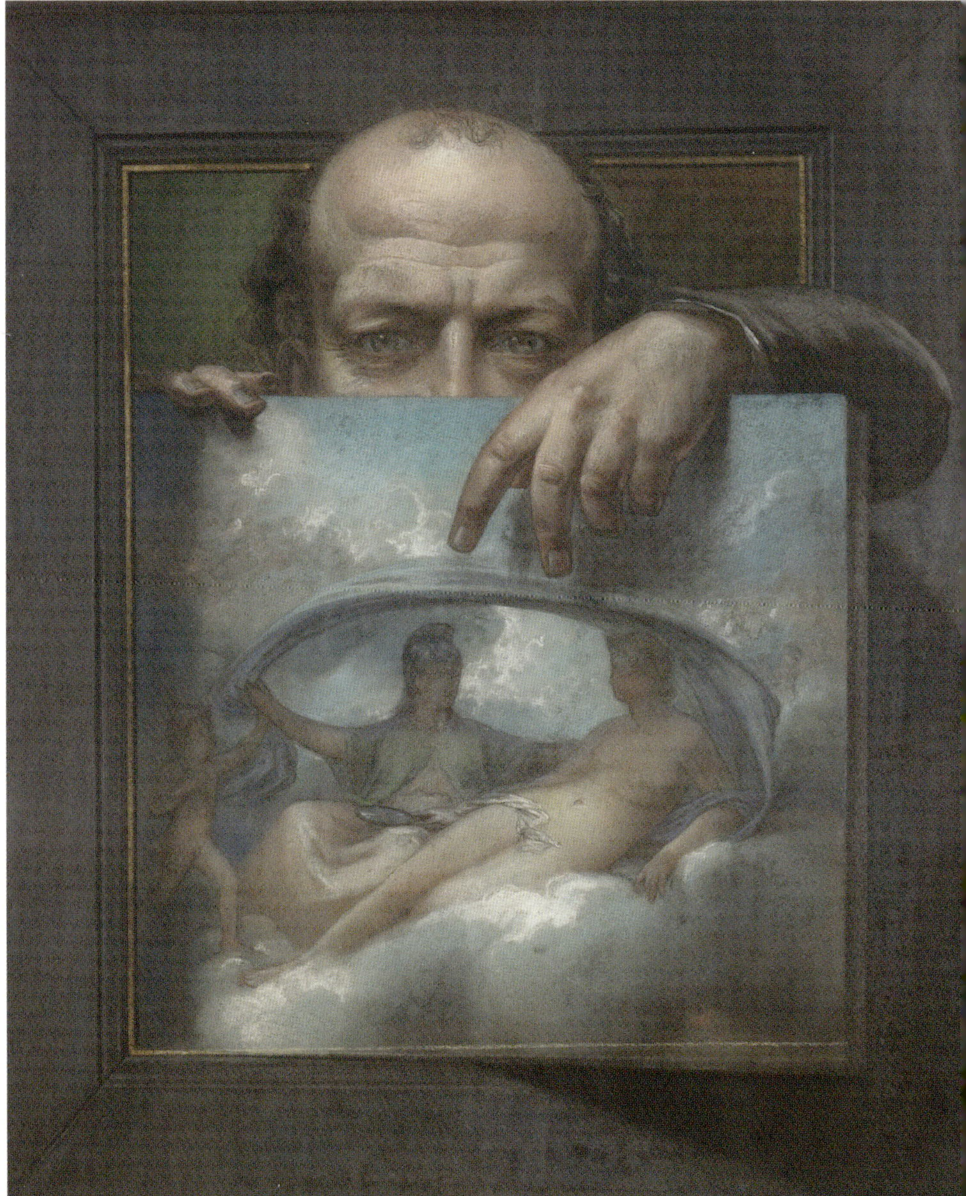

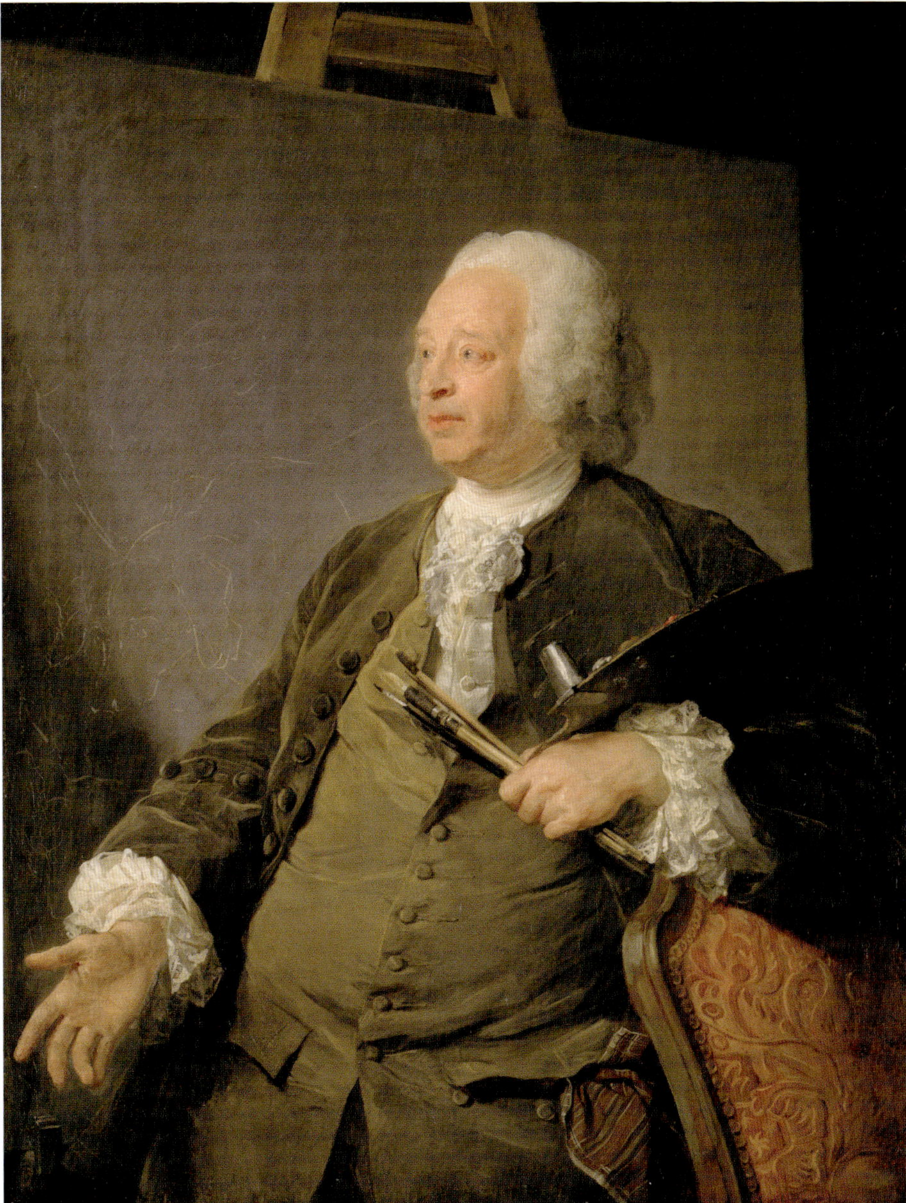

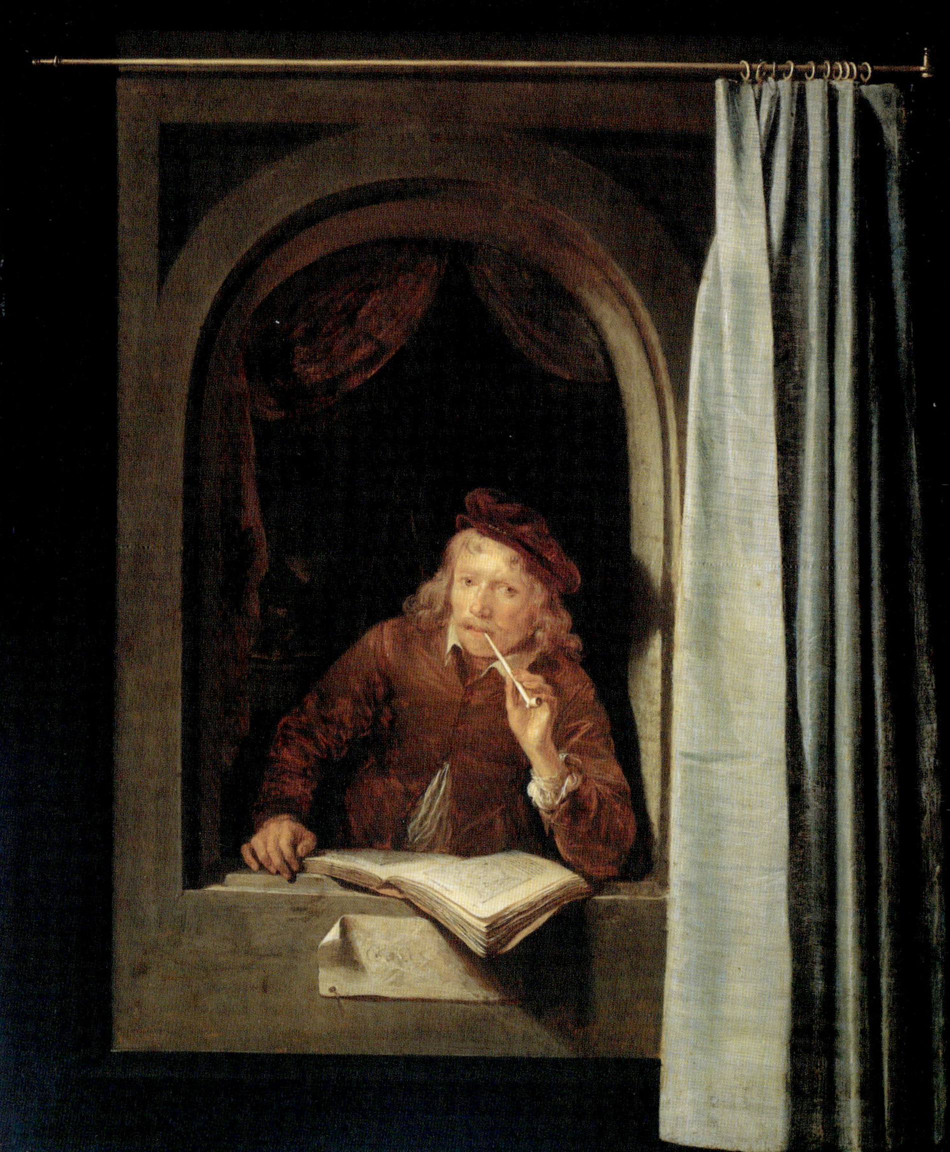

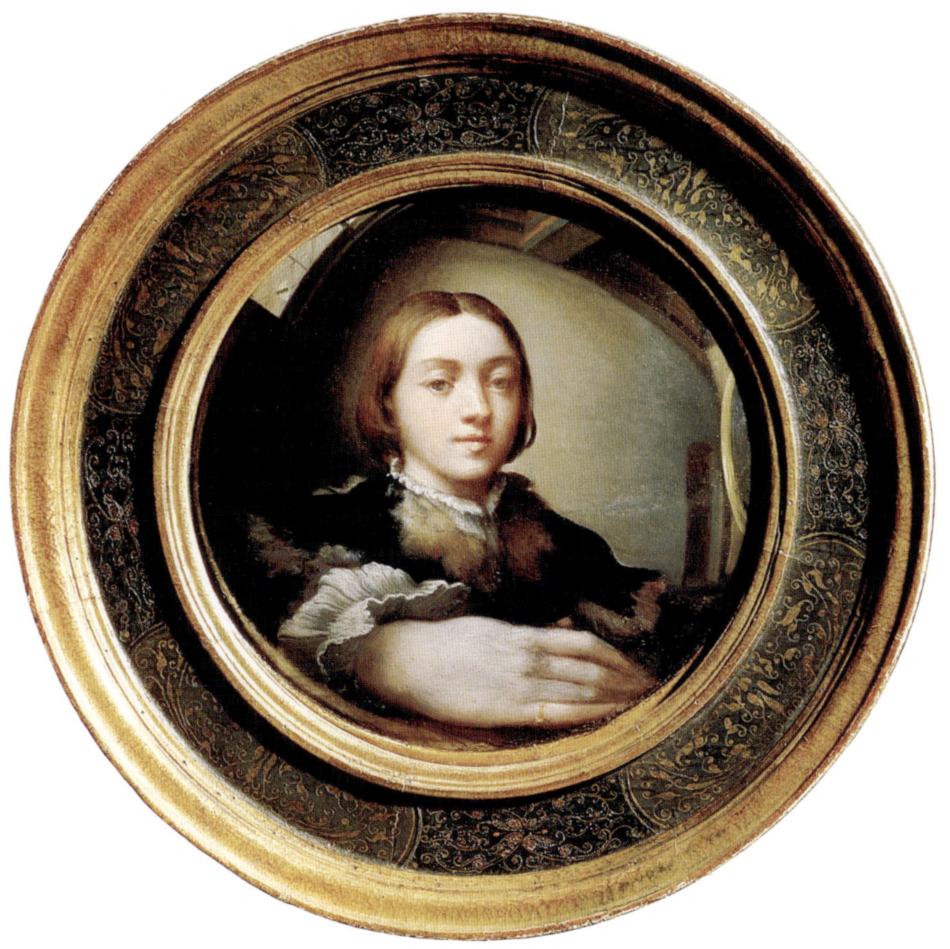

20. Gerrit Dou
Self-Portrait, circa 1650

21. Parmigianino
Self-Portrait in the Mirror,
1523

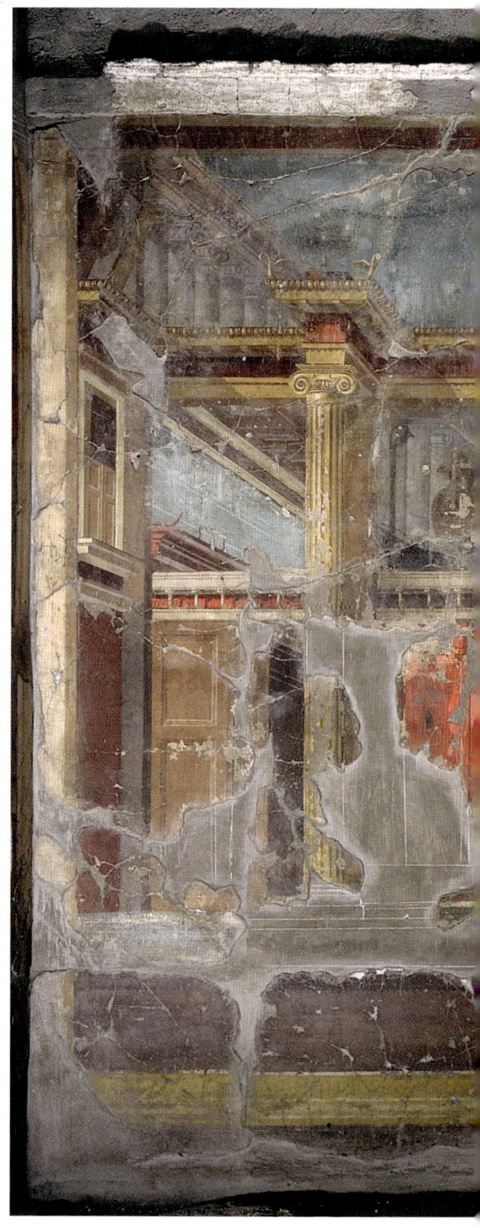

22. *Fresco in the Villa of Poppaea in Oplontis,* mid 1st century AD

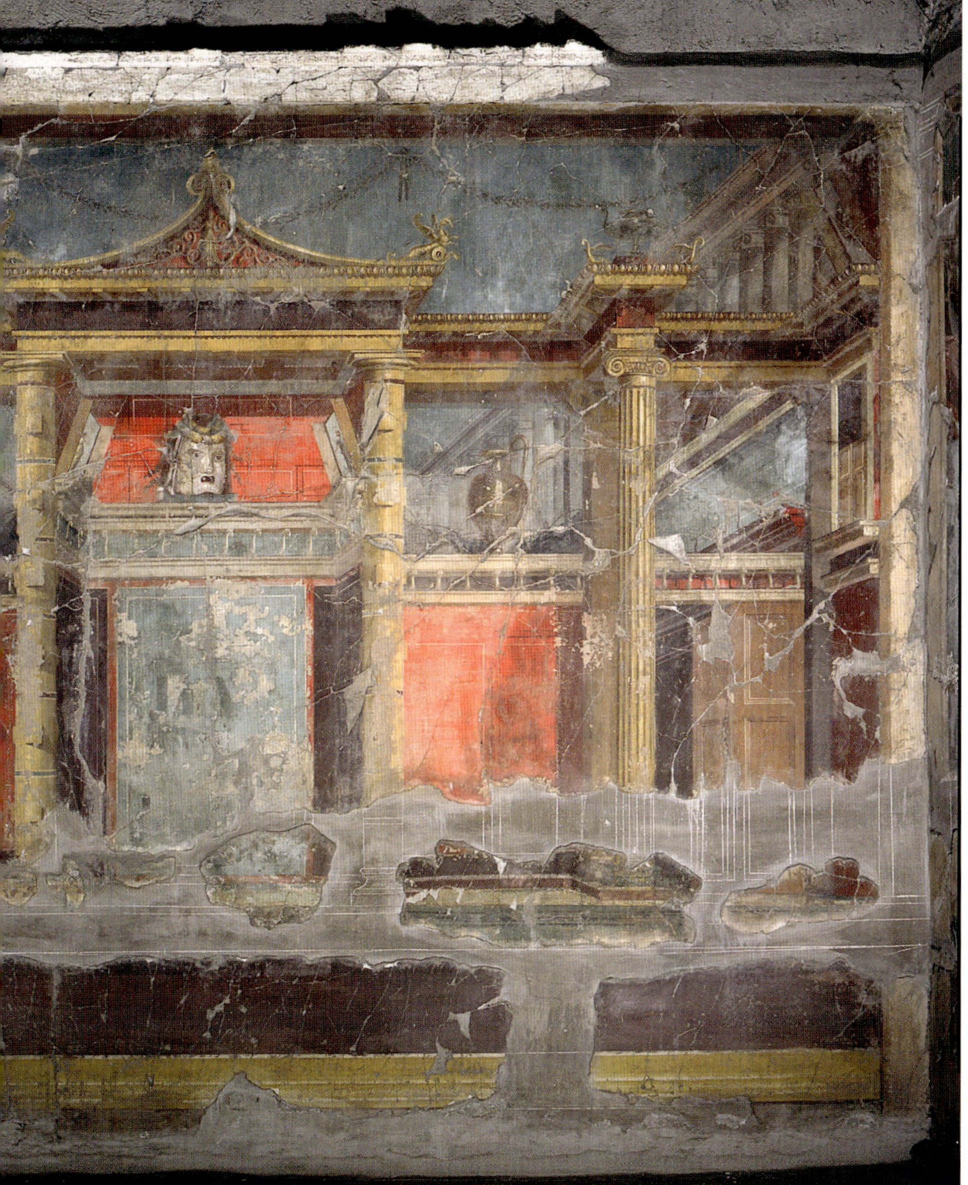

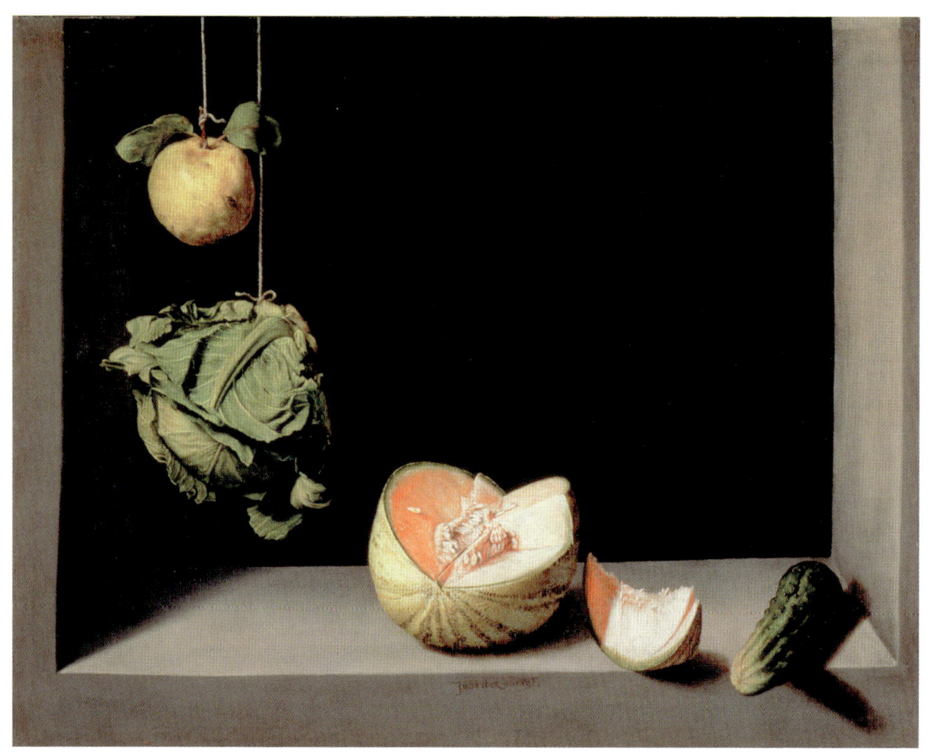

23. Juan Sánchez Cotán
*Still-life with cabbage, melon
and cucumber, ante* 1603

24. Carlo Carrà
Still-life with set-square, 1917

54

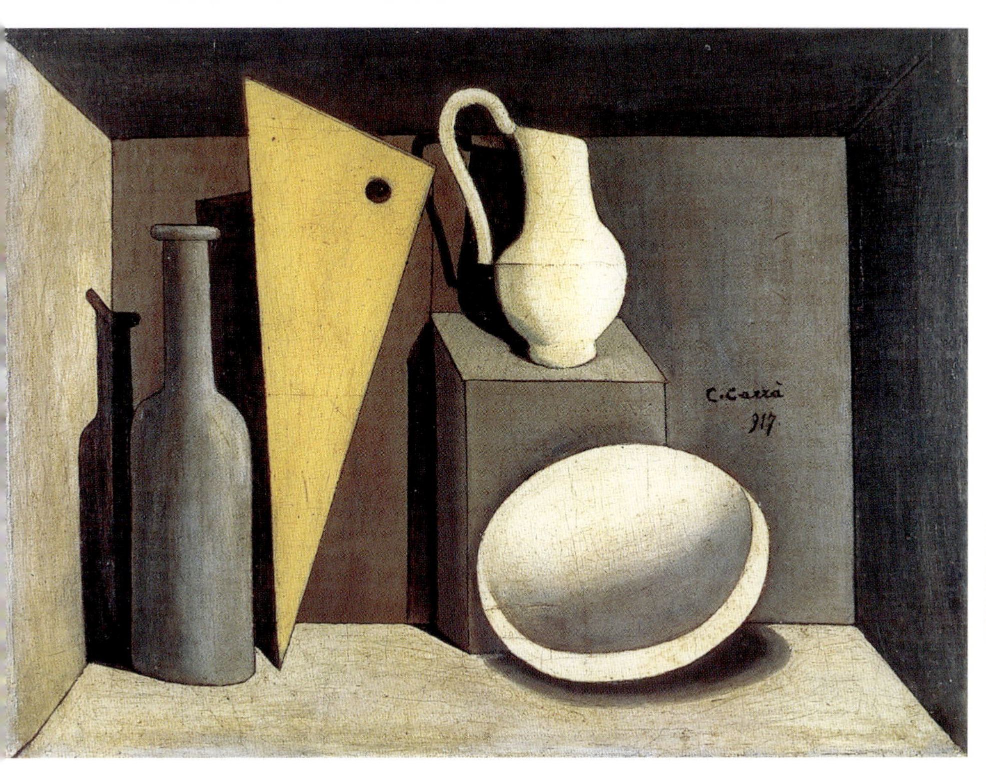

C. Carrà
917

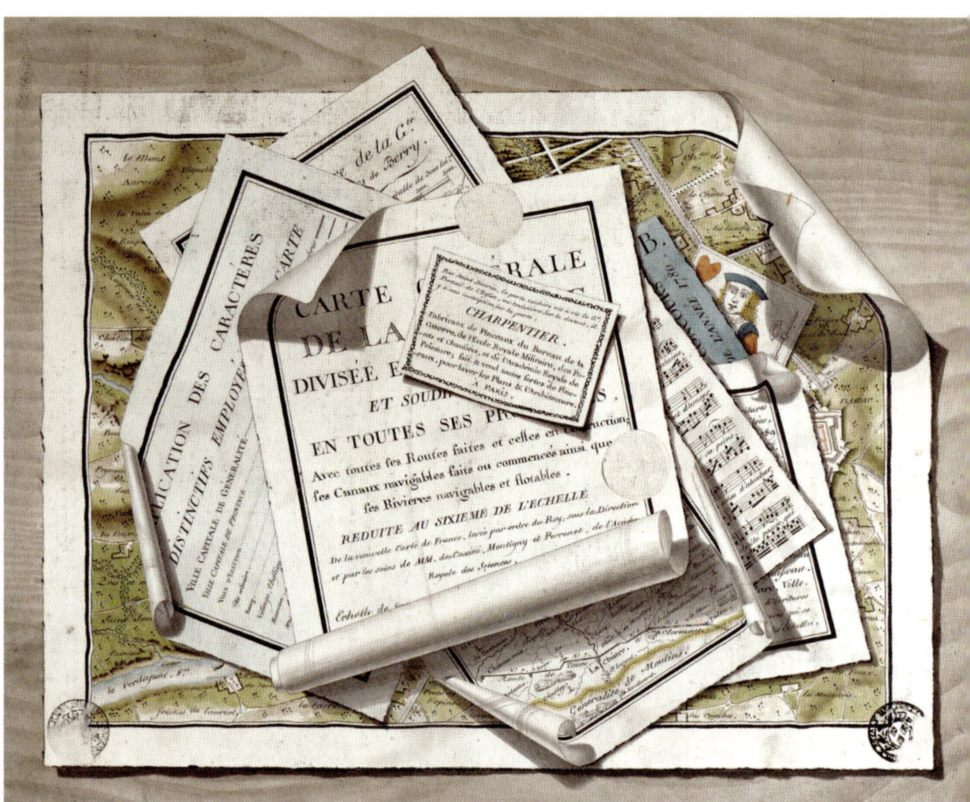

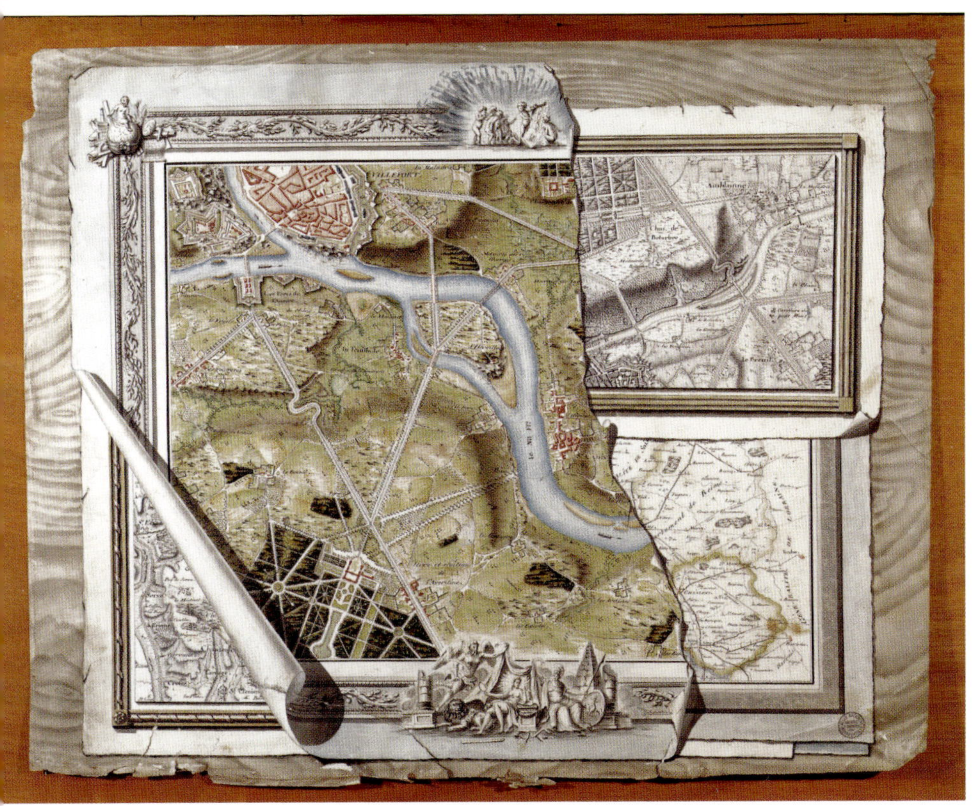

25. Anonymous
Trompe l'oeil, 18th century

26. Anonymous
Plan for four maps,
18th century

Following pages
27. Antonio Forbera
Painter's easel, 1686

28. René Magritte
La Condition humaine
(*The Human Condition*), 1933

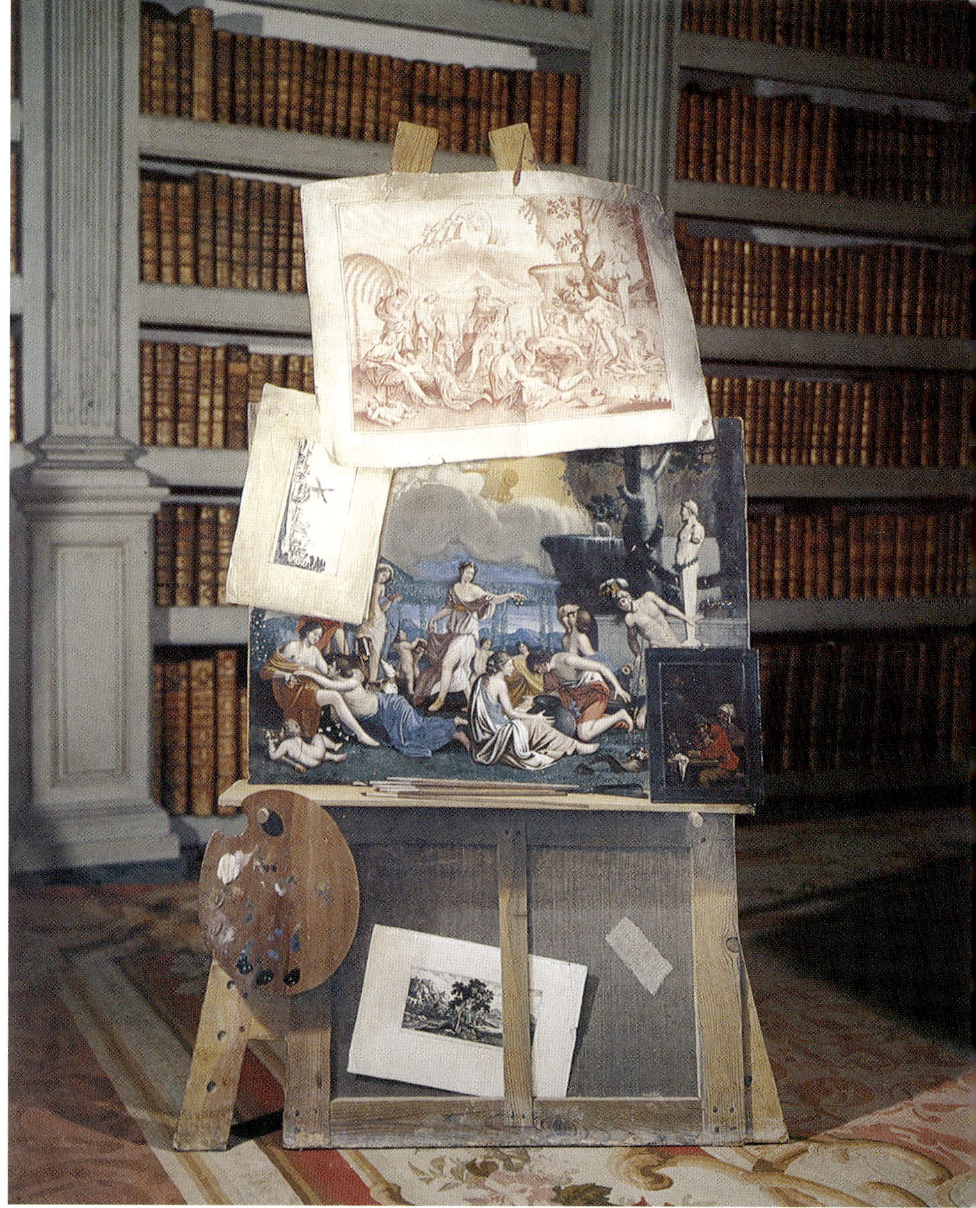

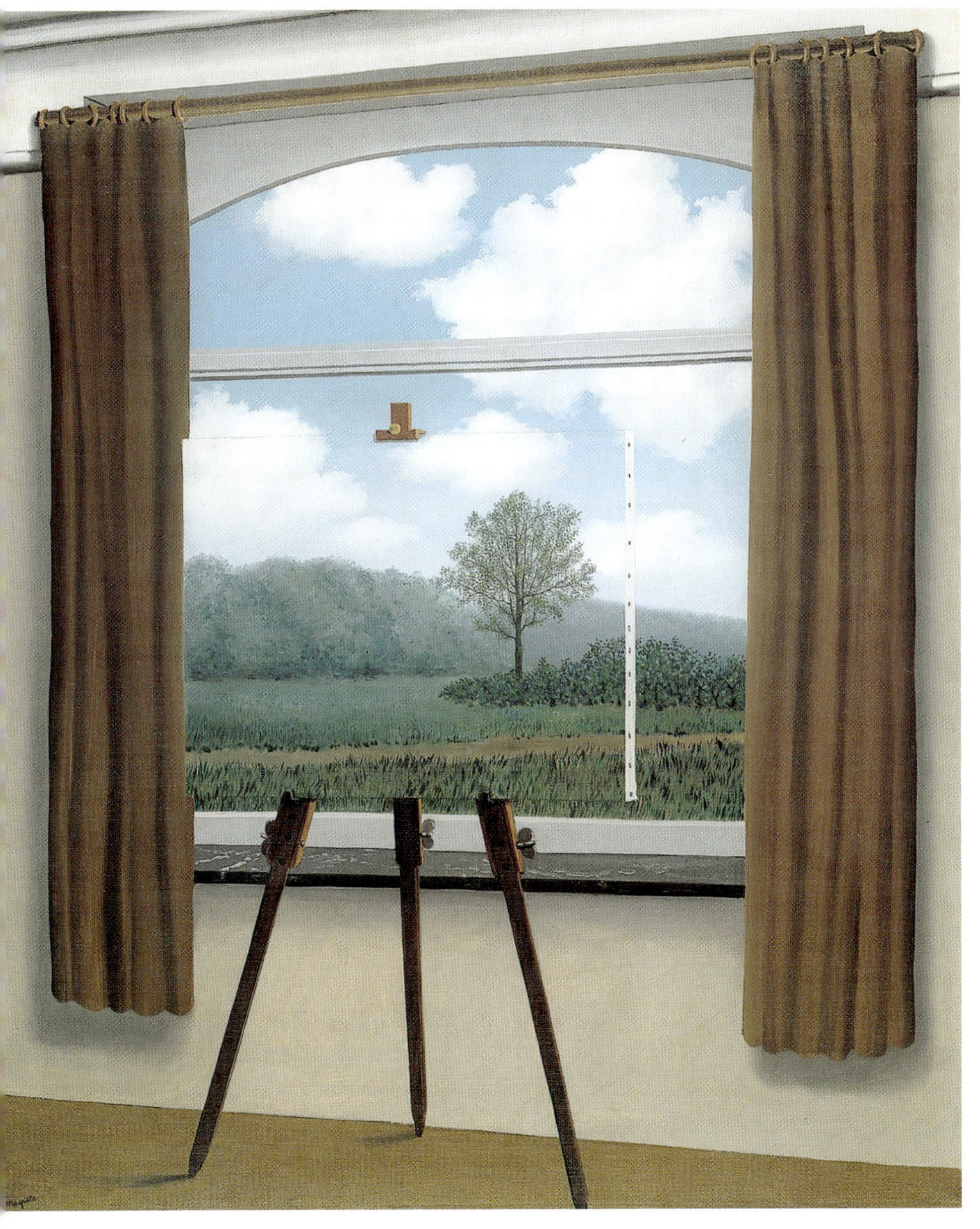

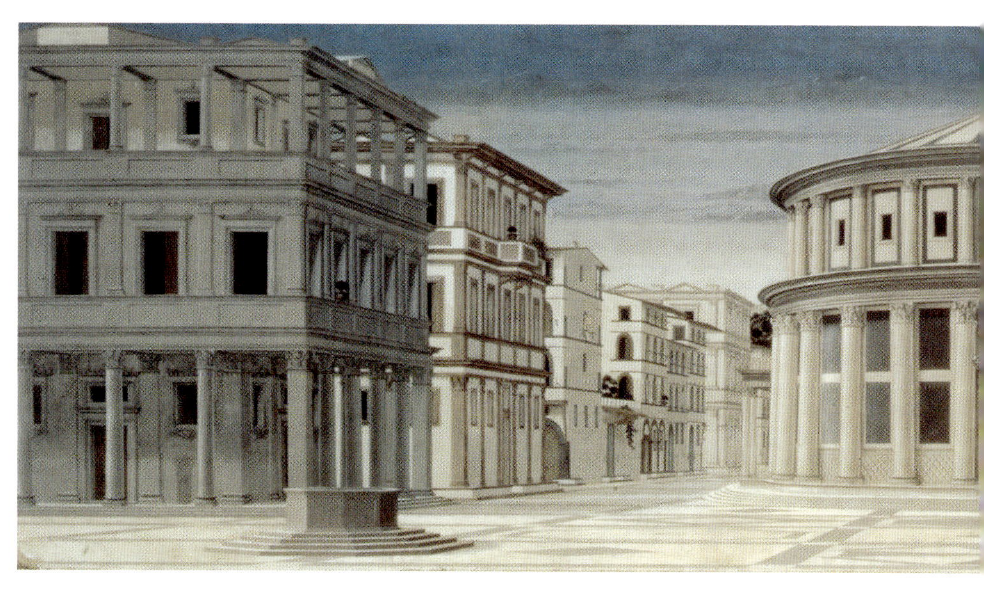

29. Luciano Laurana
Ideal city, circa 1470

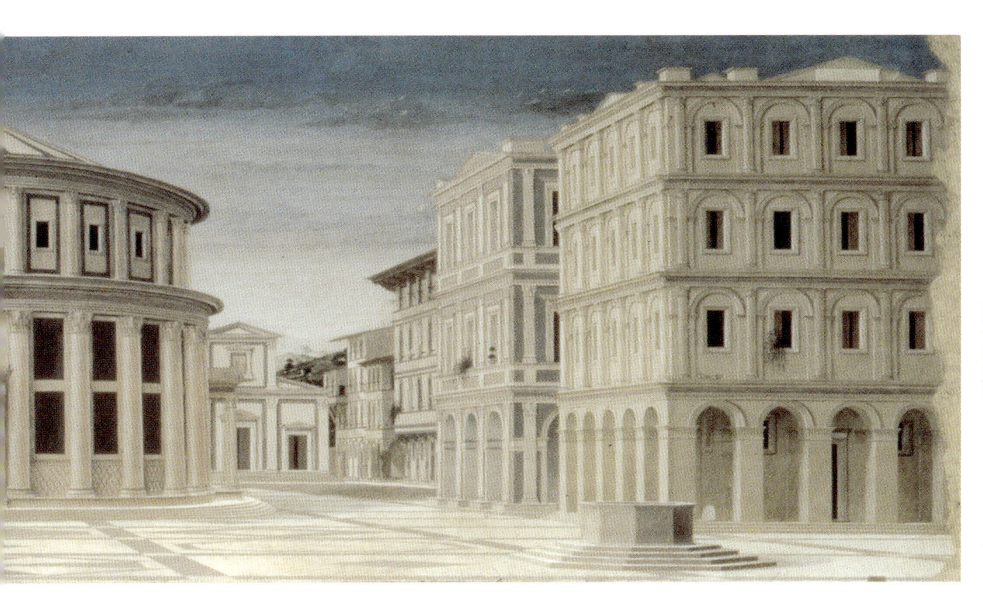

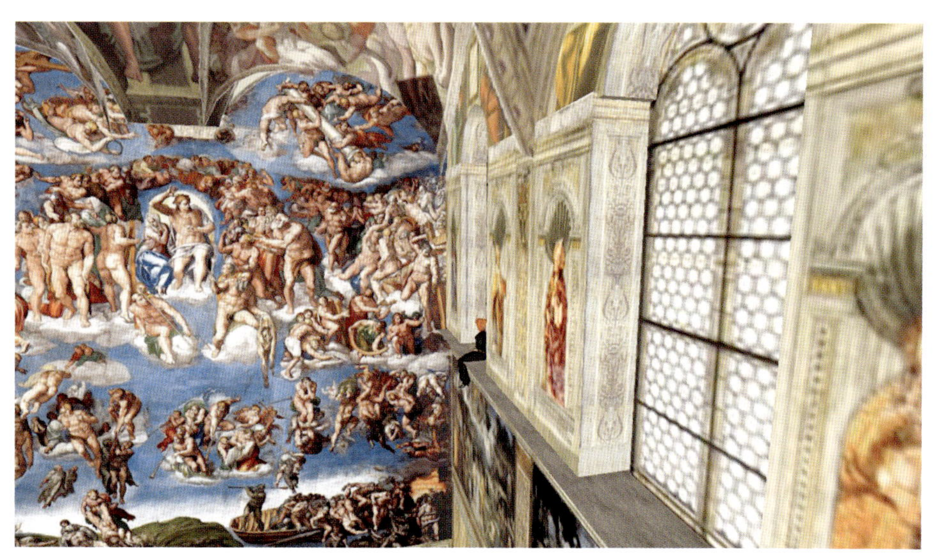

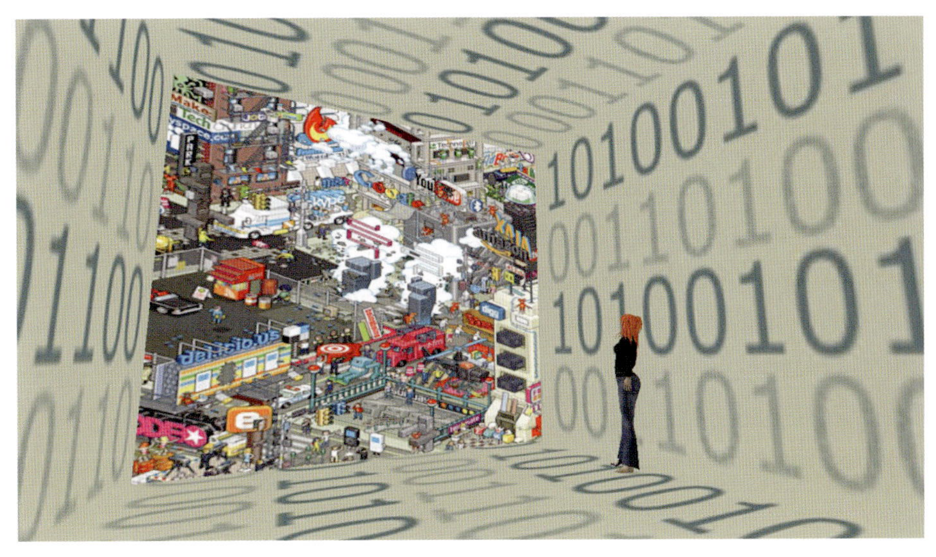

30. Second life
Sistine Chapel

31. Second life
Virtual tunnel

Following pages
32. *Unswept floor,*
1st century AD

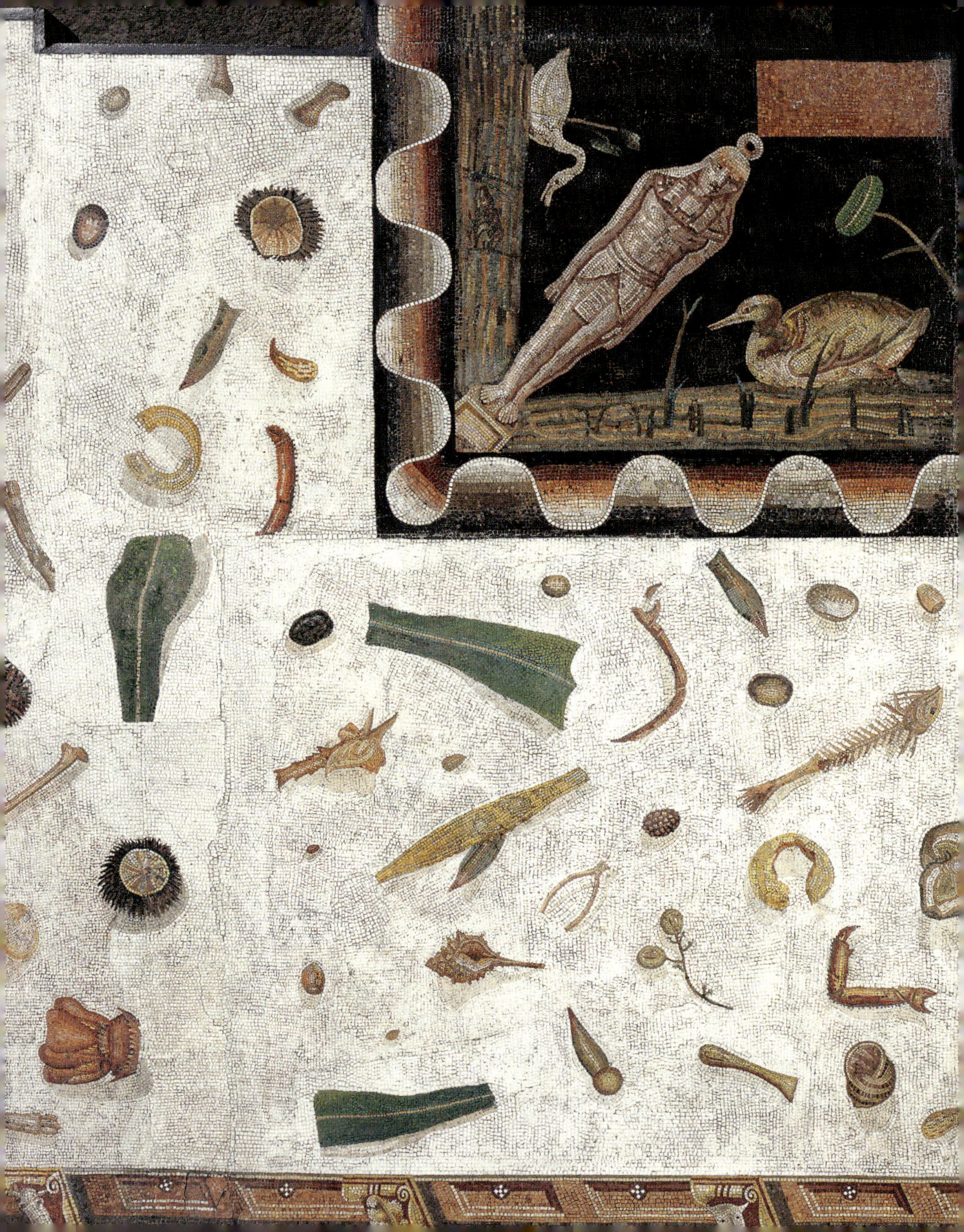

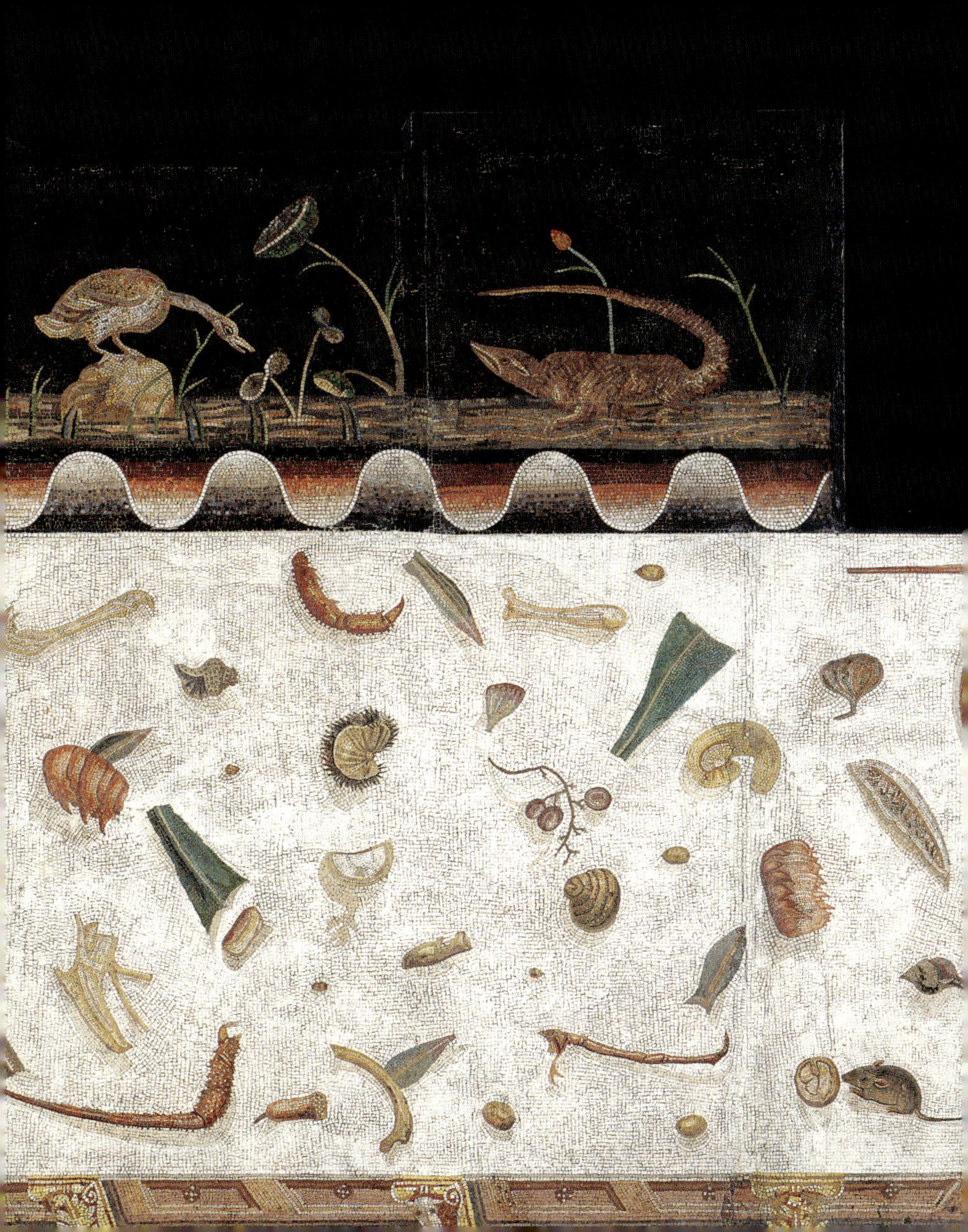

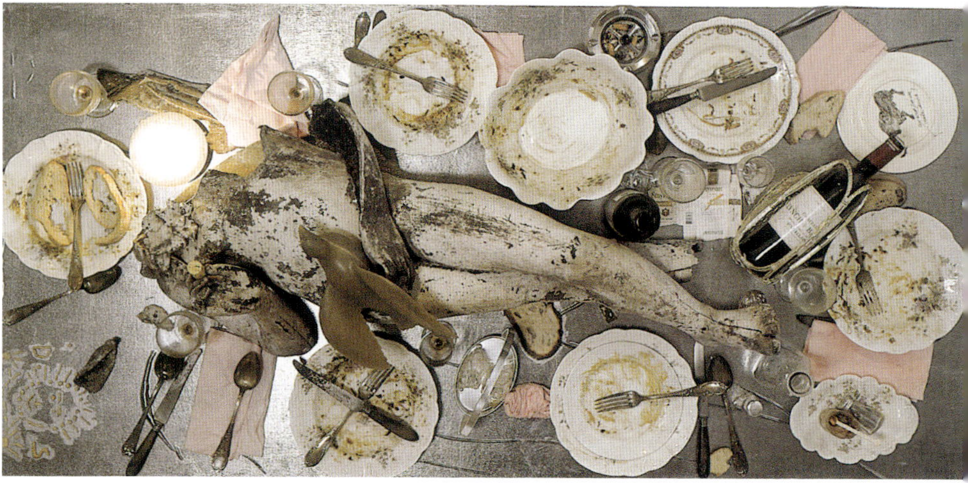

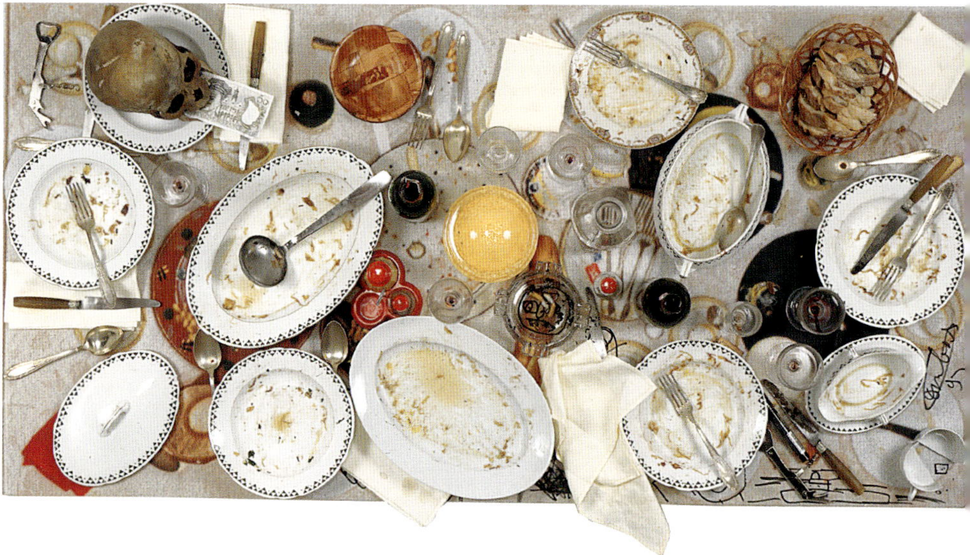

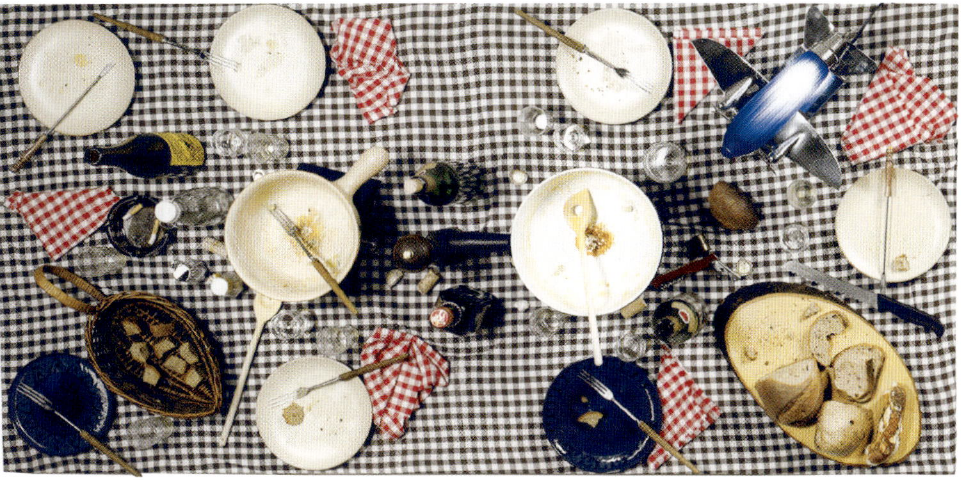

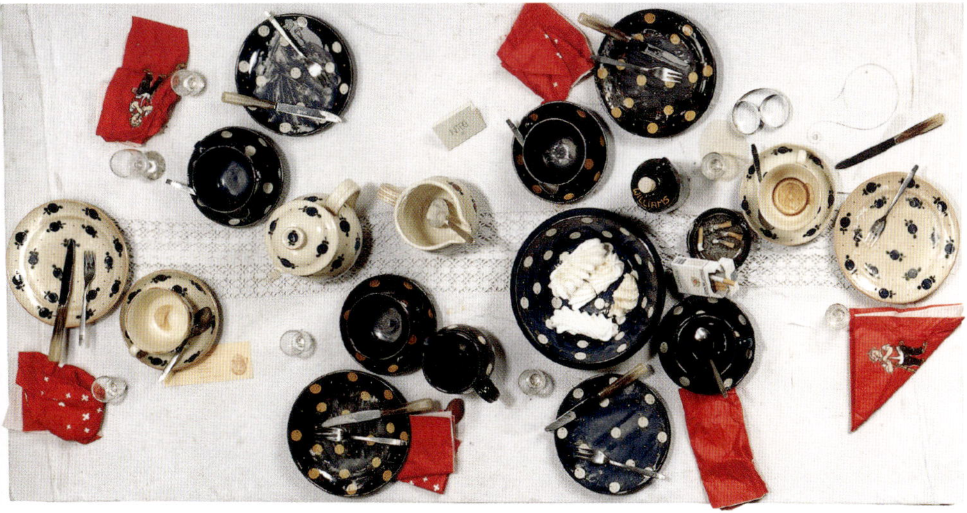

33. Daniel Spoerri
*Seville Series no. 4
and no. 12*, 1991

34. Daniel Spoerri
*Seville Series no. 3
and no. 6*, 1991

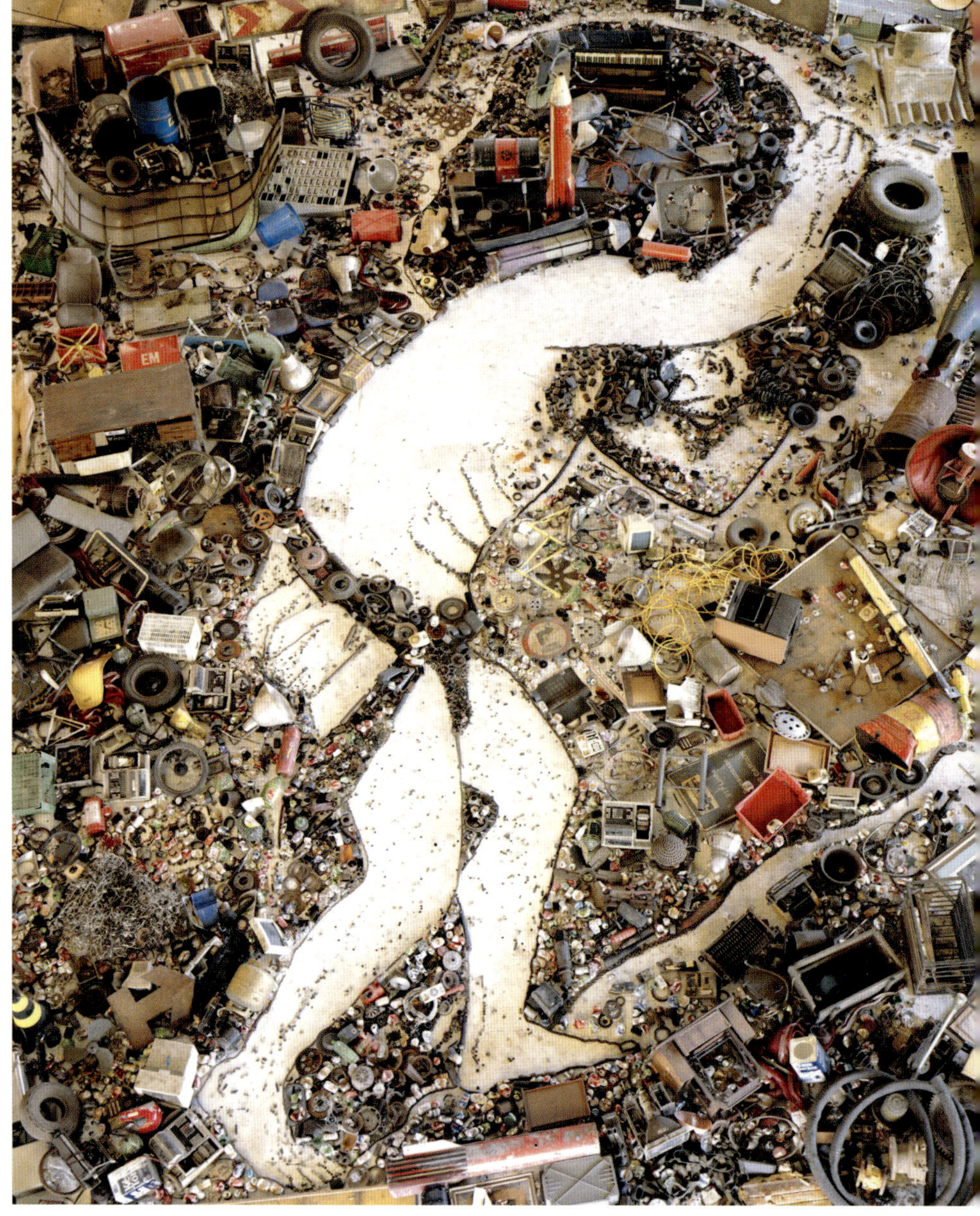

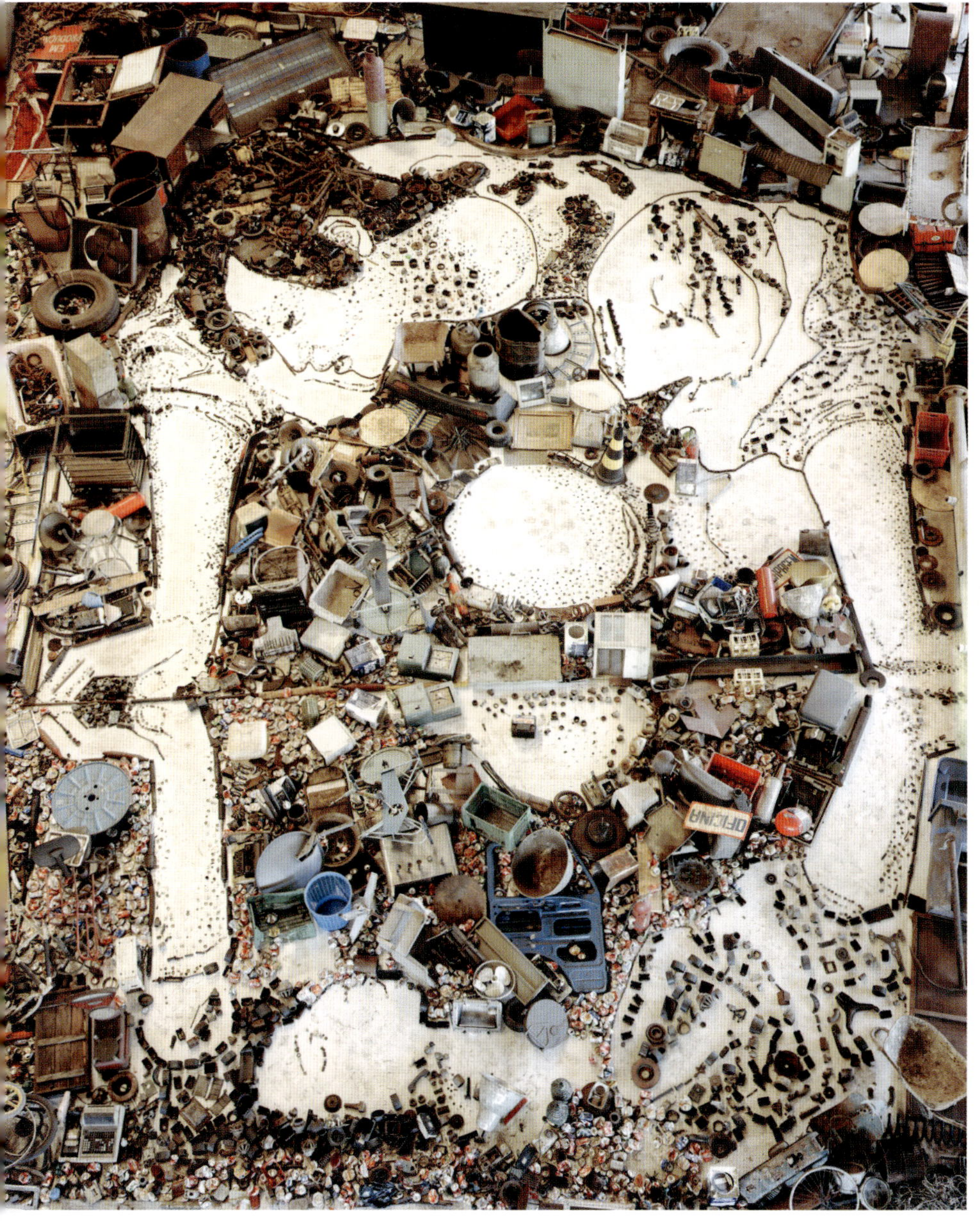
OFICINA

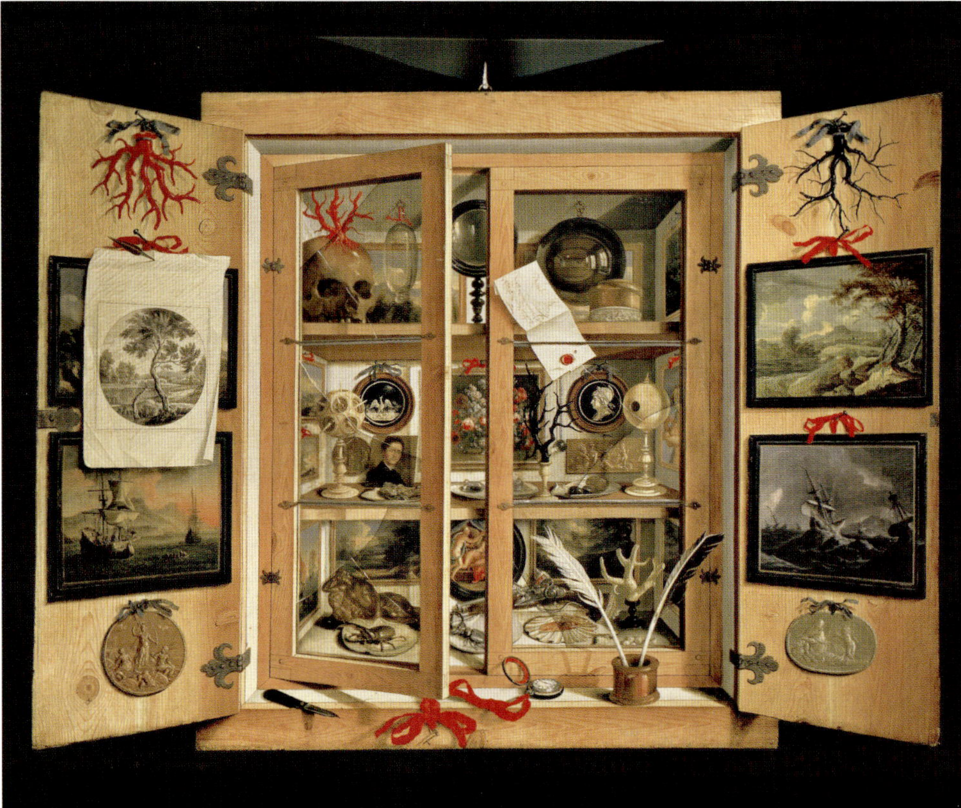

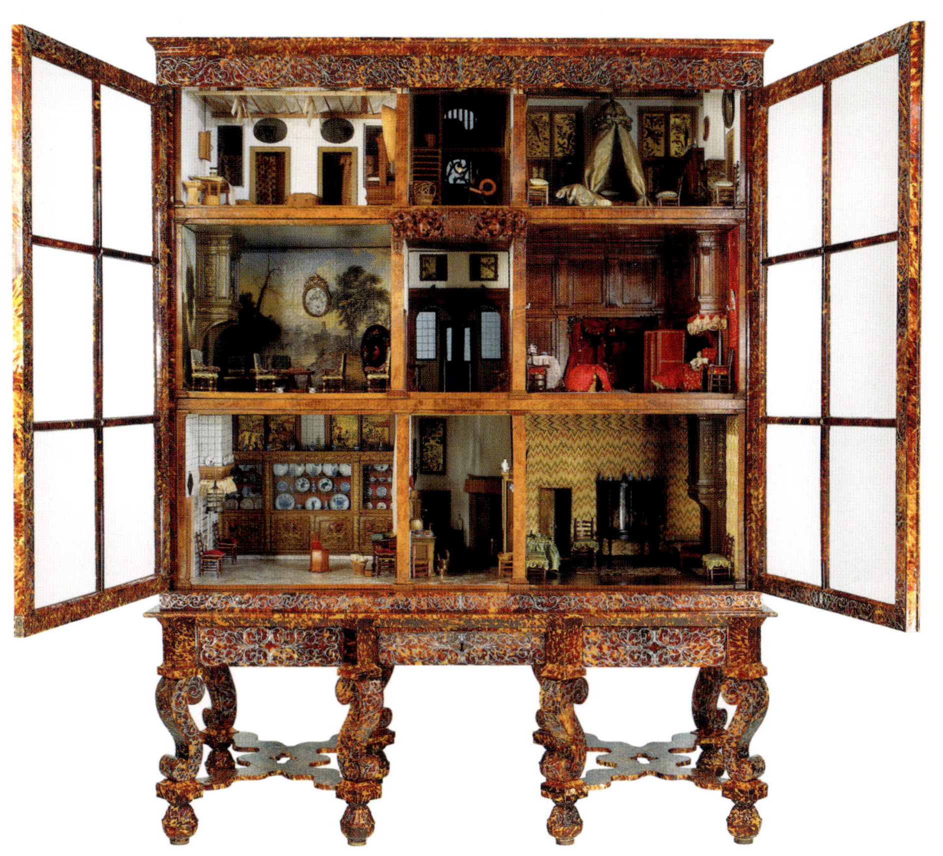

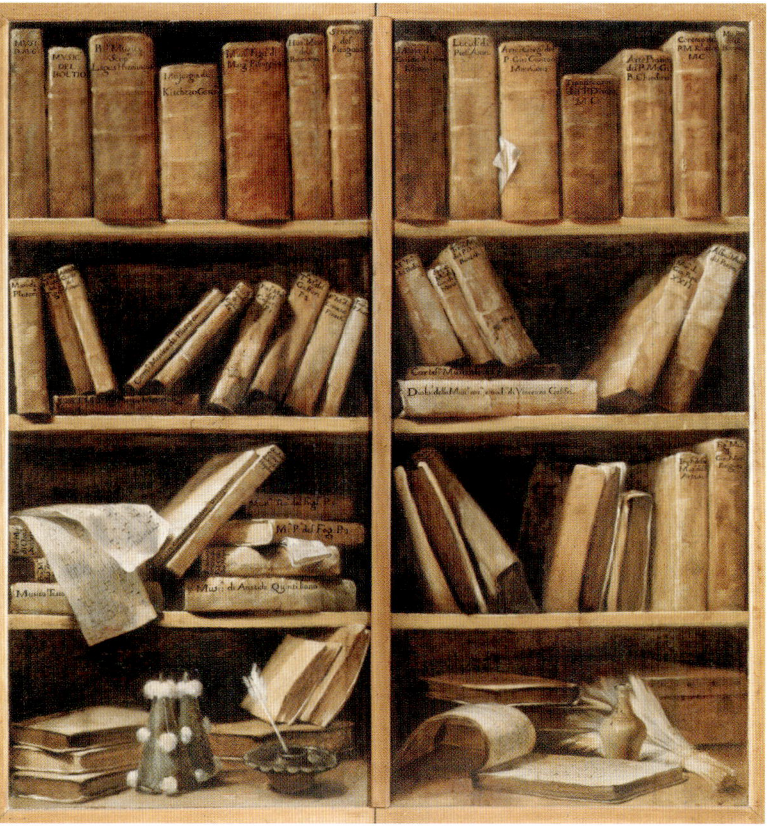

39. Giuseppe Maria Crespi
Shelves with music books,
circa 1725

40. *Wood inlay from Federico*
da Montefeltro's study,
15th century

72

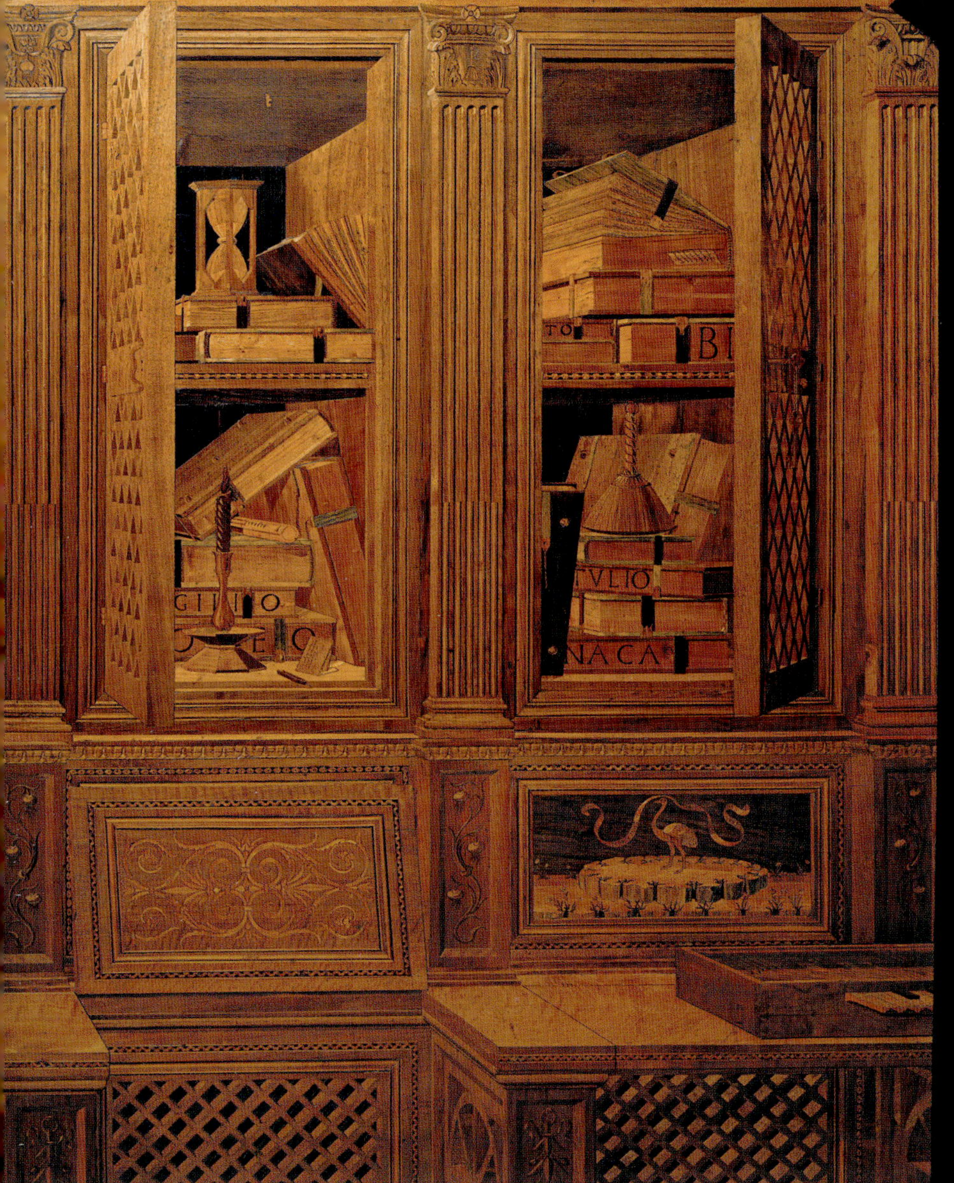
GILIO
...E C
BI
TO
VLIO
NACA

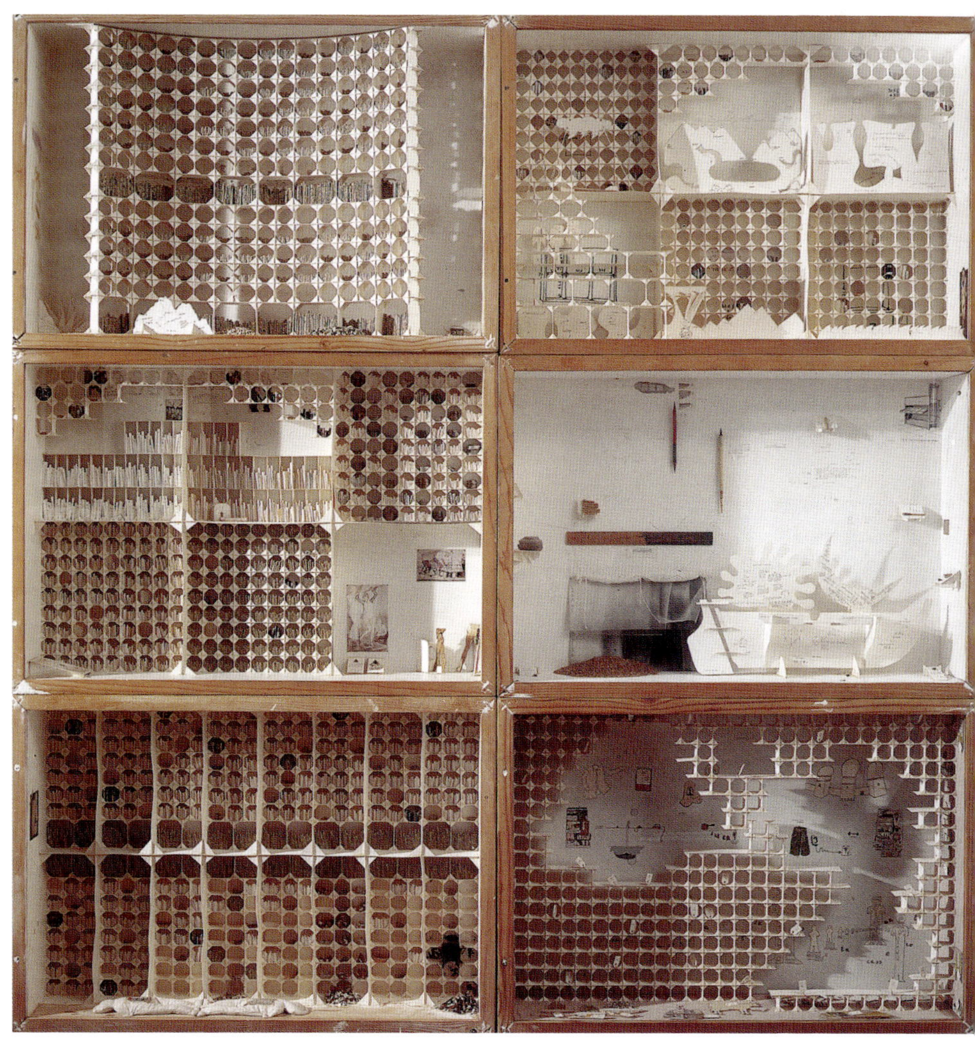

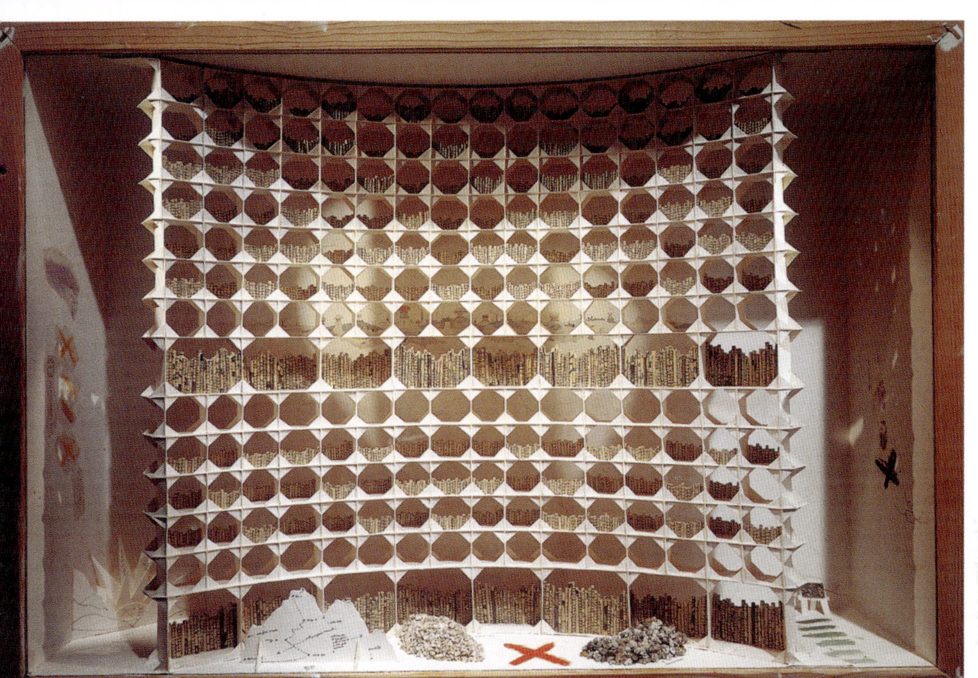

Following pages

42. Pieter von Balthasar
Wall paper mimesis, 2007

43. Pieter von Balthasar
Wall paper mimesis, 2007

41. Gianfranco Baruchello
The Big Library (full view
and detail), 1976-86

75

Wall paper mimesis

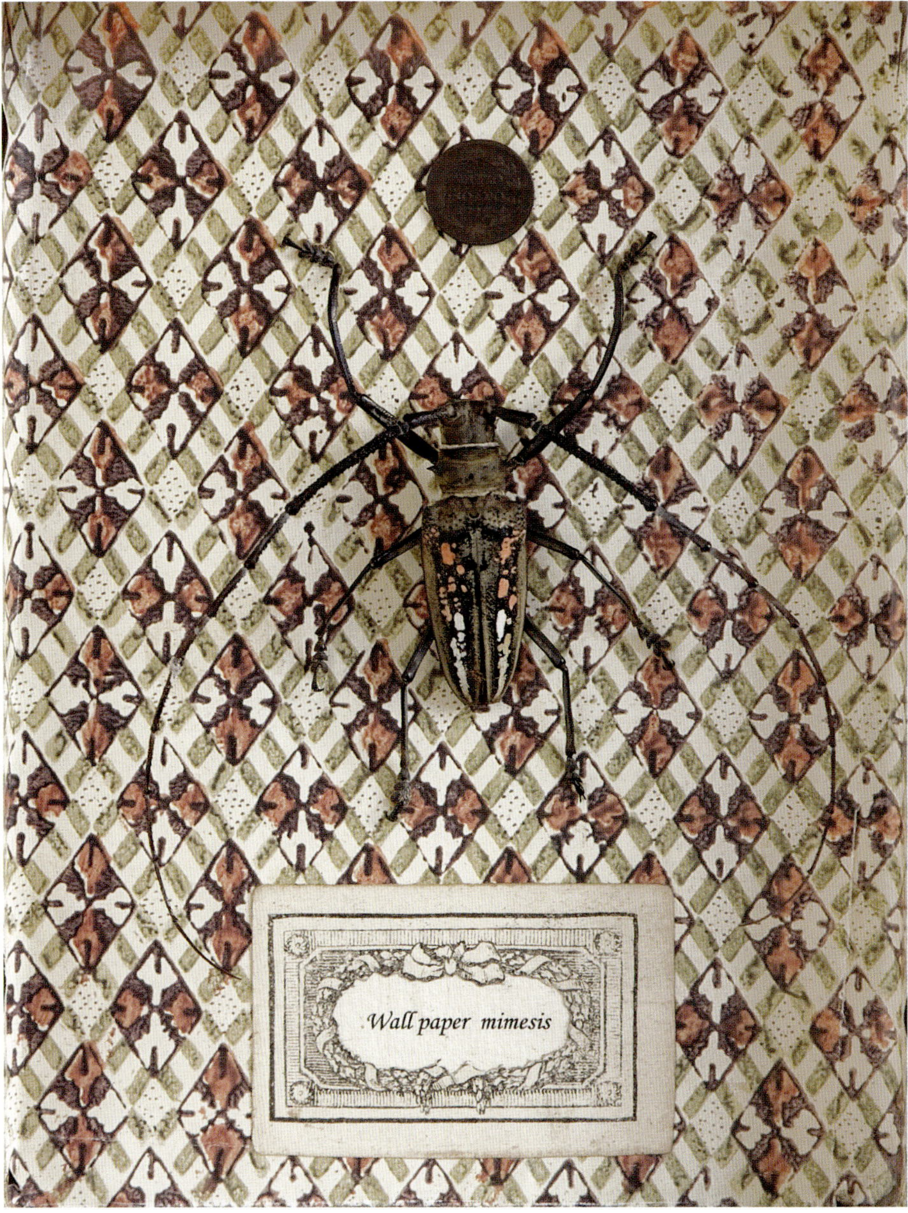
Wall paper mimesis

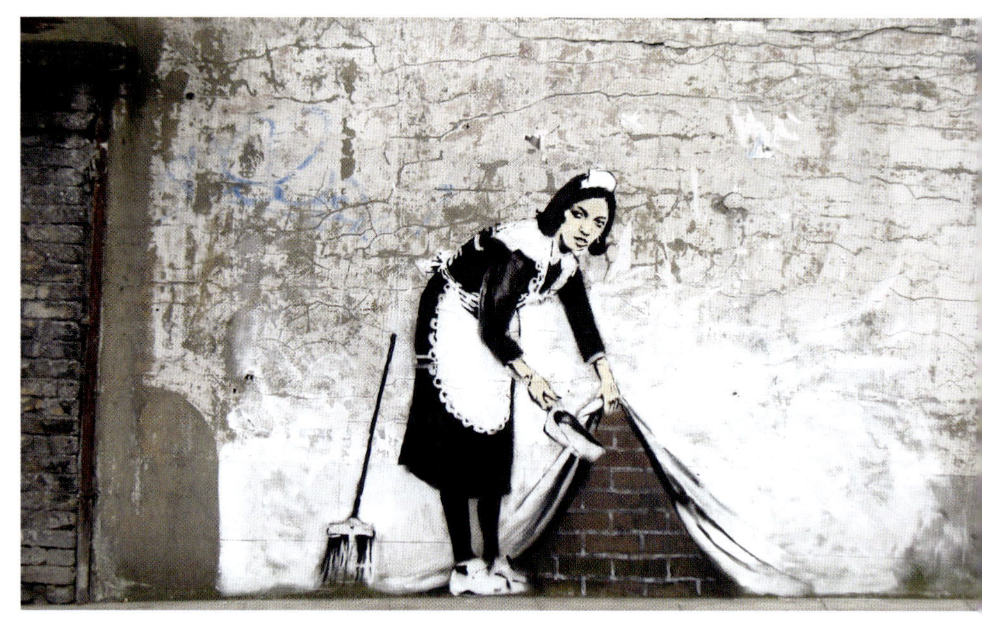

44. Banksy
Sweep at Hoxton, circa 2001

**45. Michelangelo
Pistoletto**
Man repairing a truck, 1967

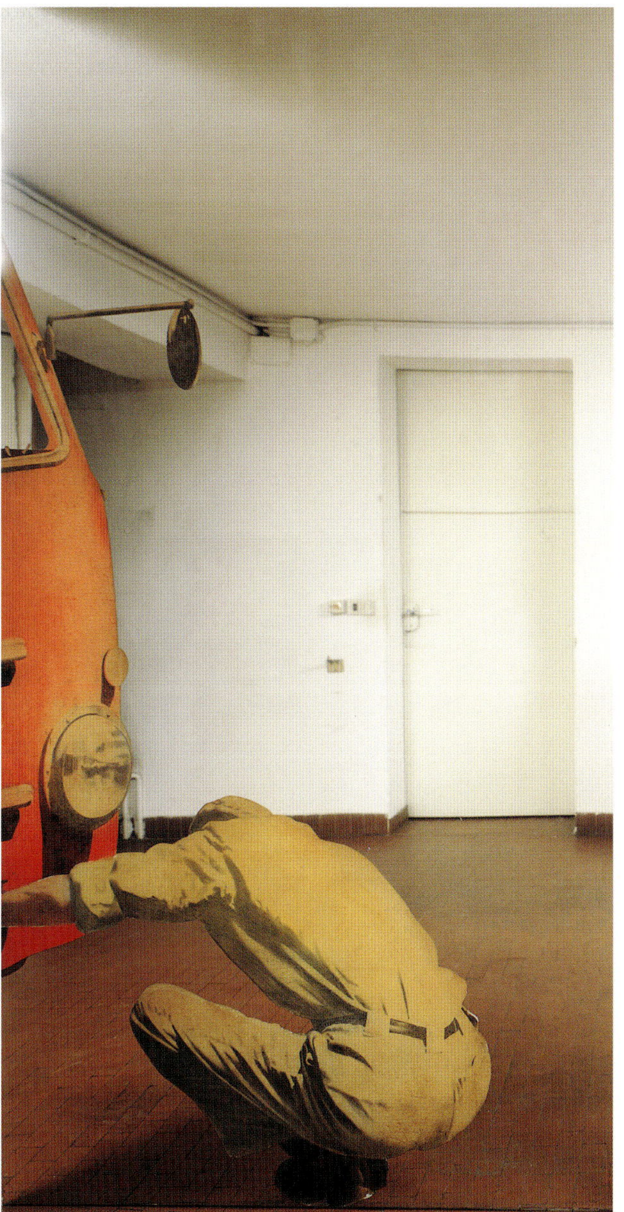

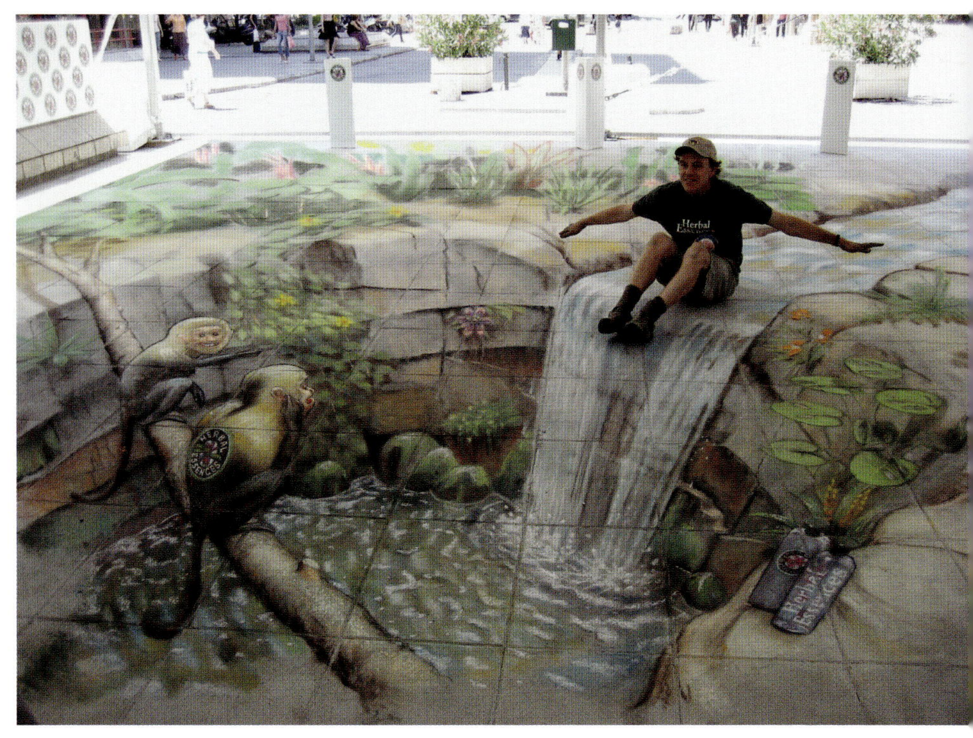

Following pages
48. William Cochran
A handful of keys

46. Julian Beever
Madrid, 2007

49. Duane Hanson
Housewife, 1969-70

47. Domenico Ghirlandaio
*Stories of John the Baptist,
Visitation* (detail), 1485-90

50. Duane Hanson
Homeless, 1991

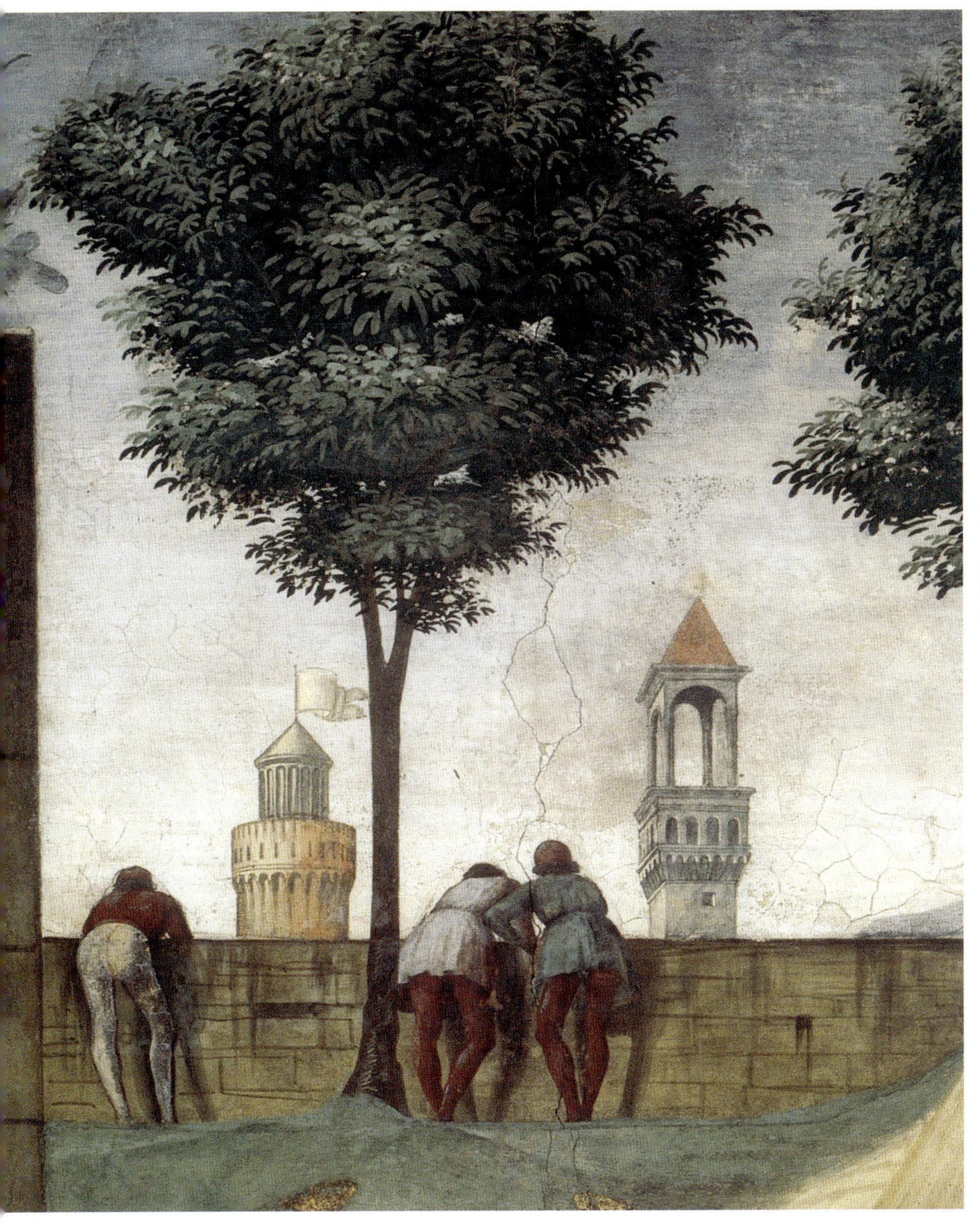

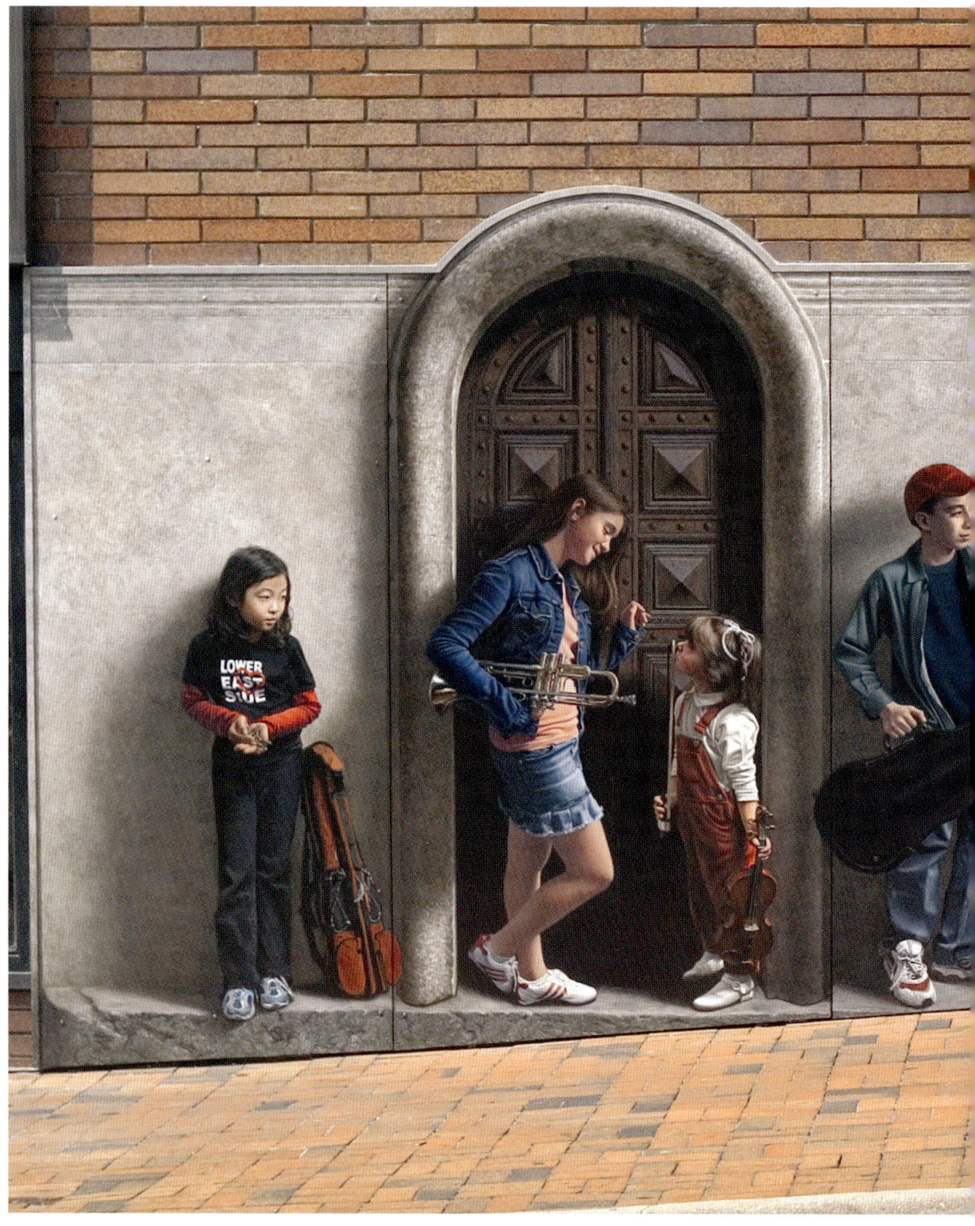

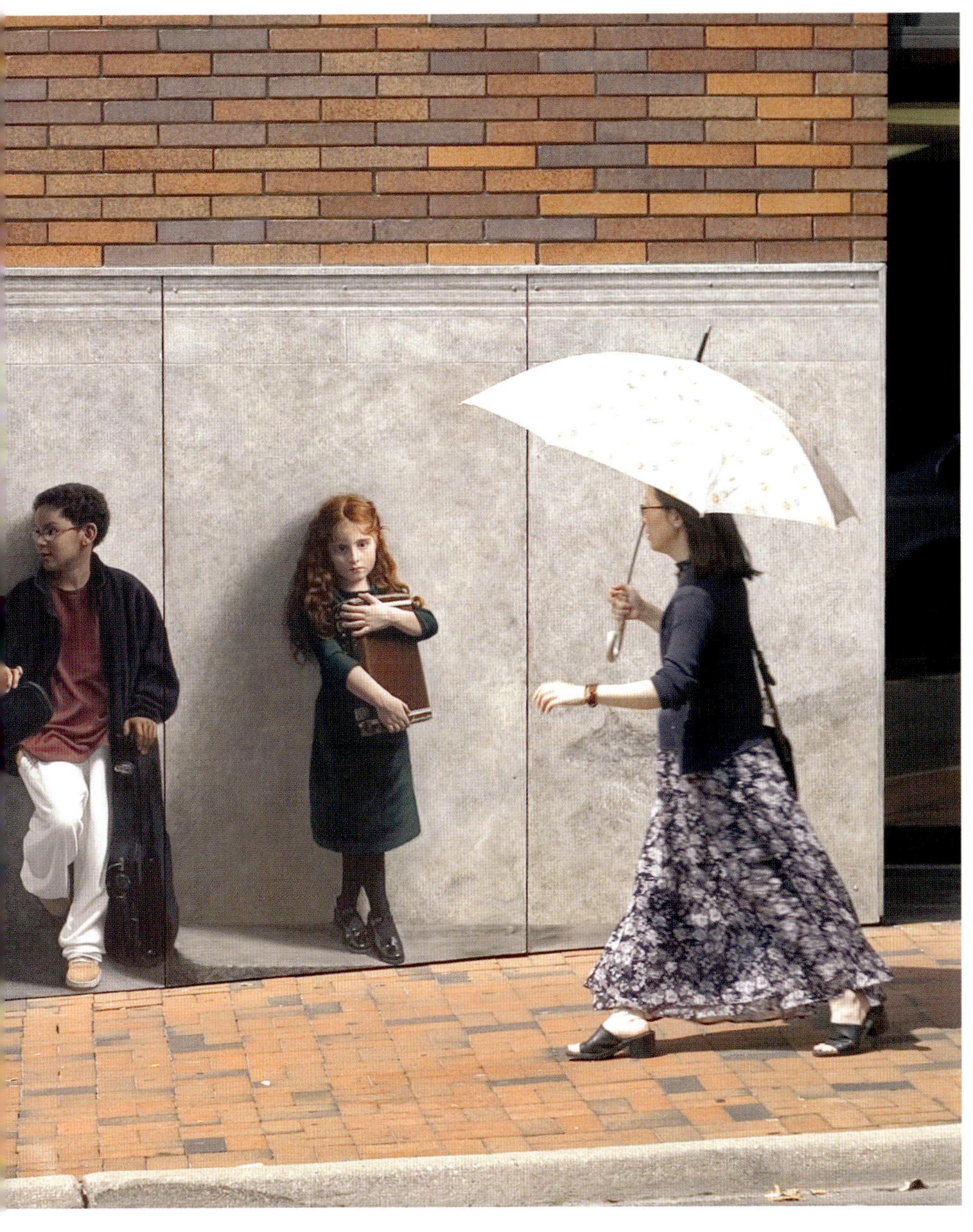

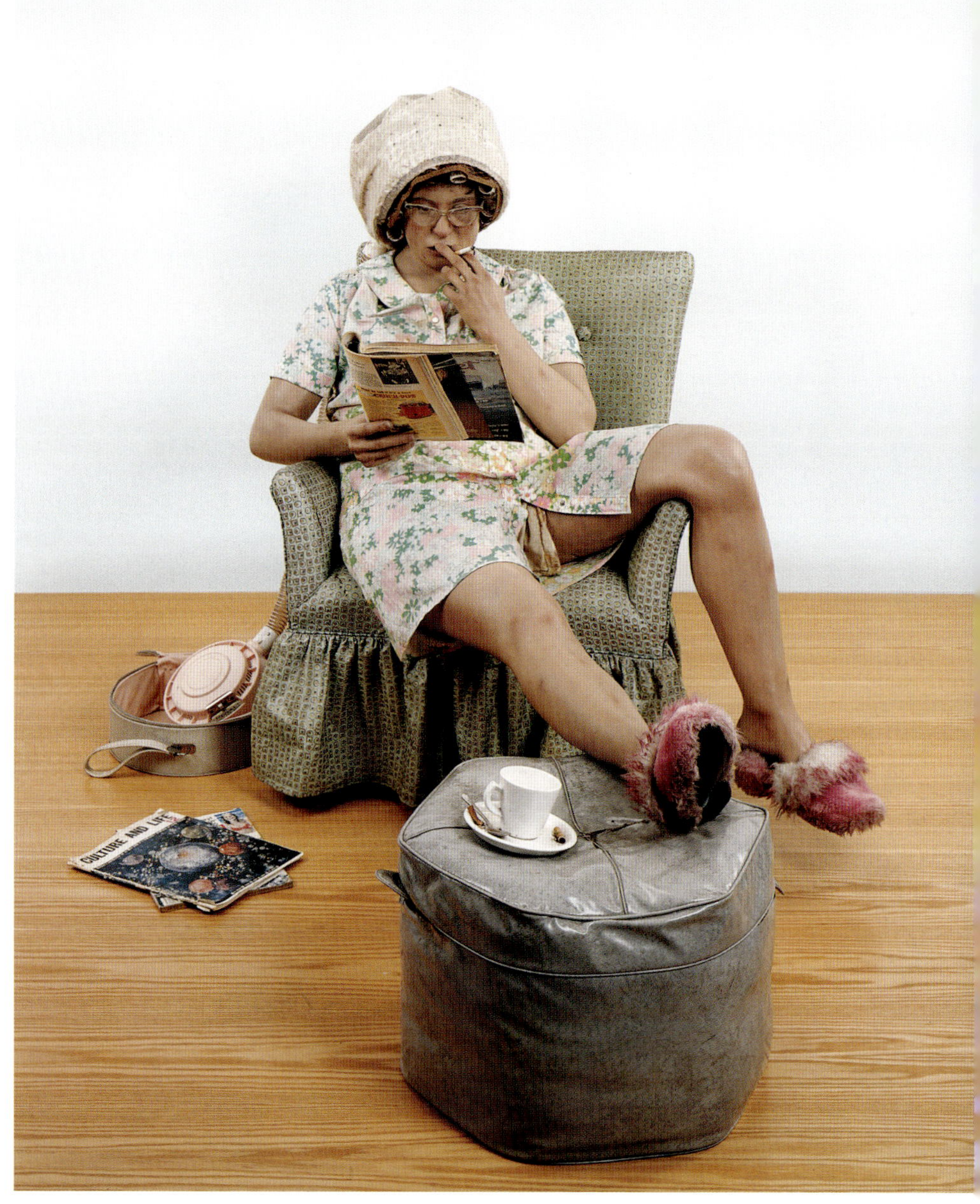

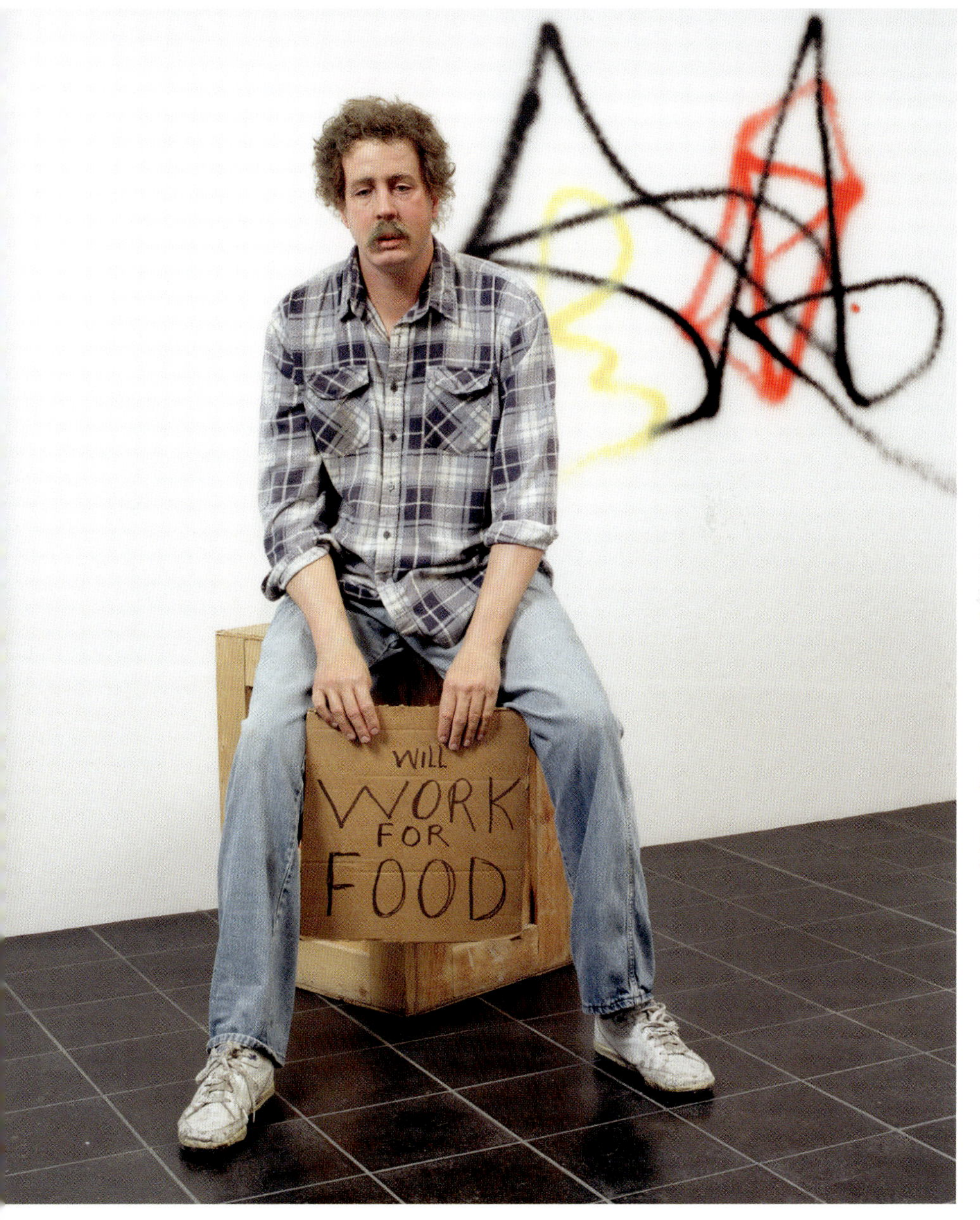

WILL
WORK
FOR
FOOD

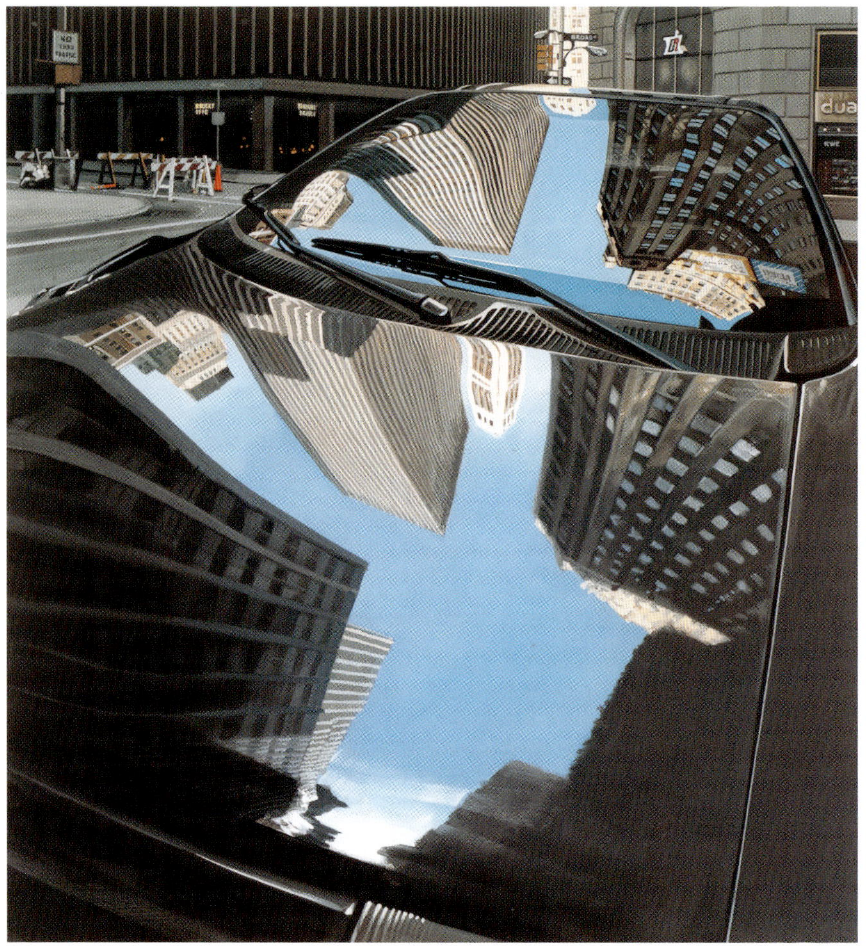

51. Richard Estes
Broad Street NYC, 2003

52. Richard Haas
Crossroads Building, Times Square, New York City, 1980

Following pages
53. Richard Estes
Times Square, 2004

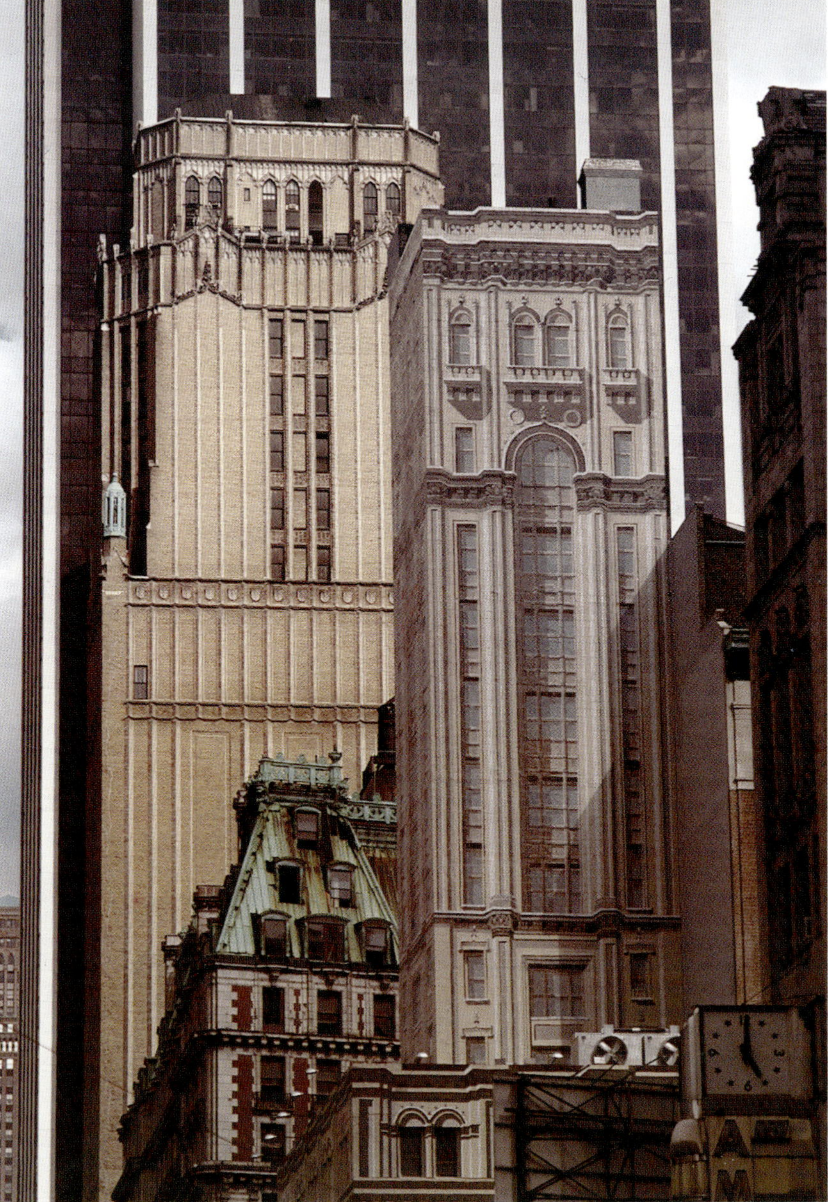

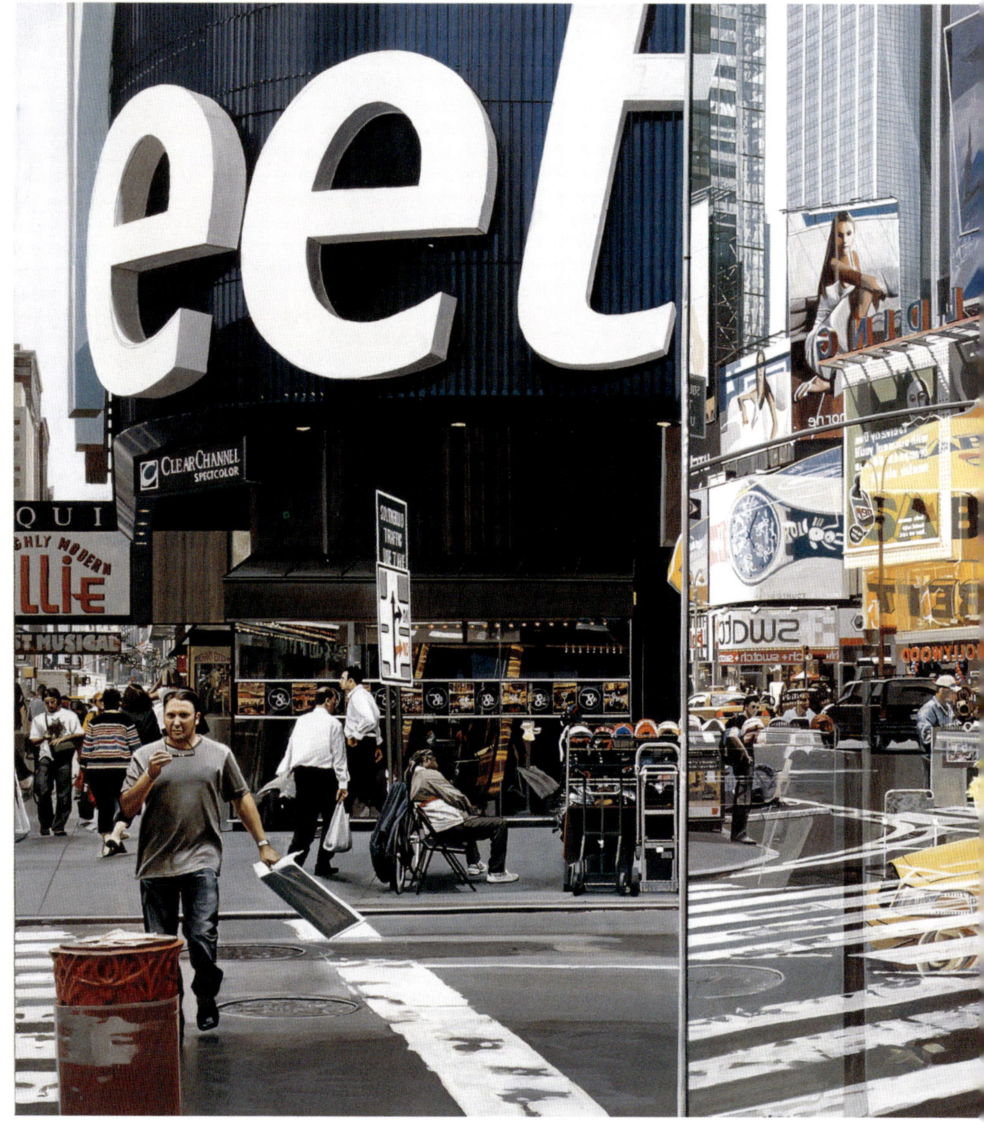
eet
CLEAR CHANNEL
SPECTCOLOR
SWatch
HOLLYWOOD
QUI
GHLY MODERN
LLIE
ST MUSICAL

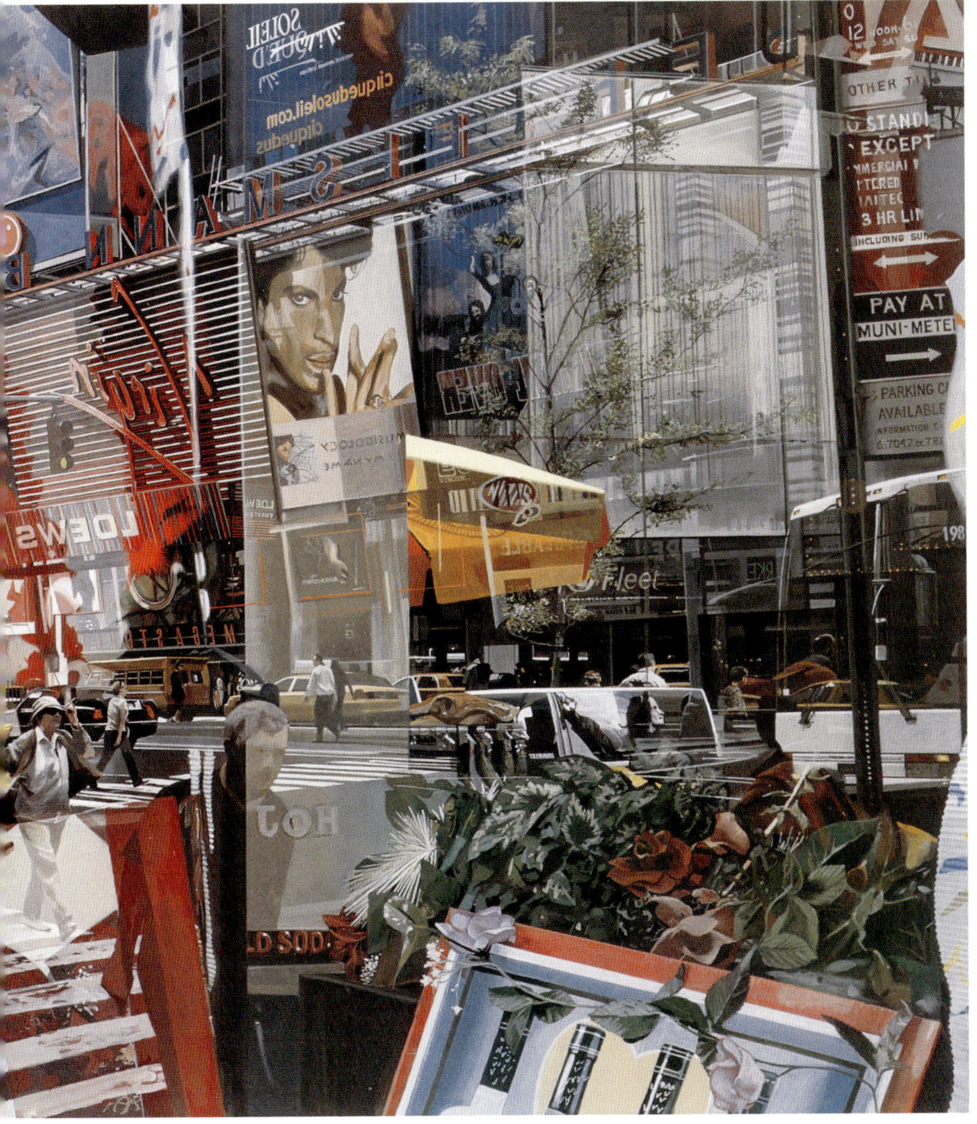

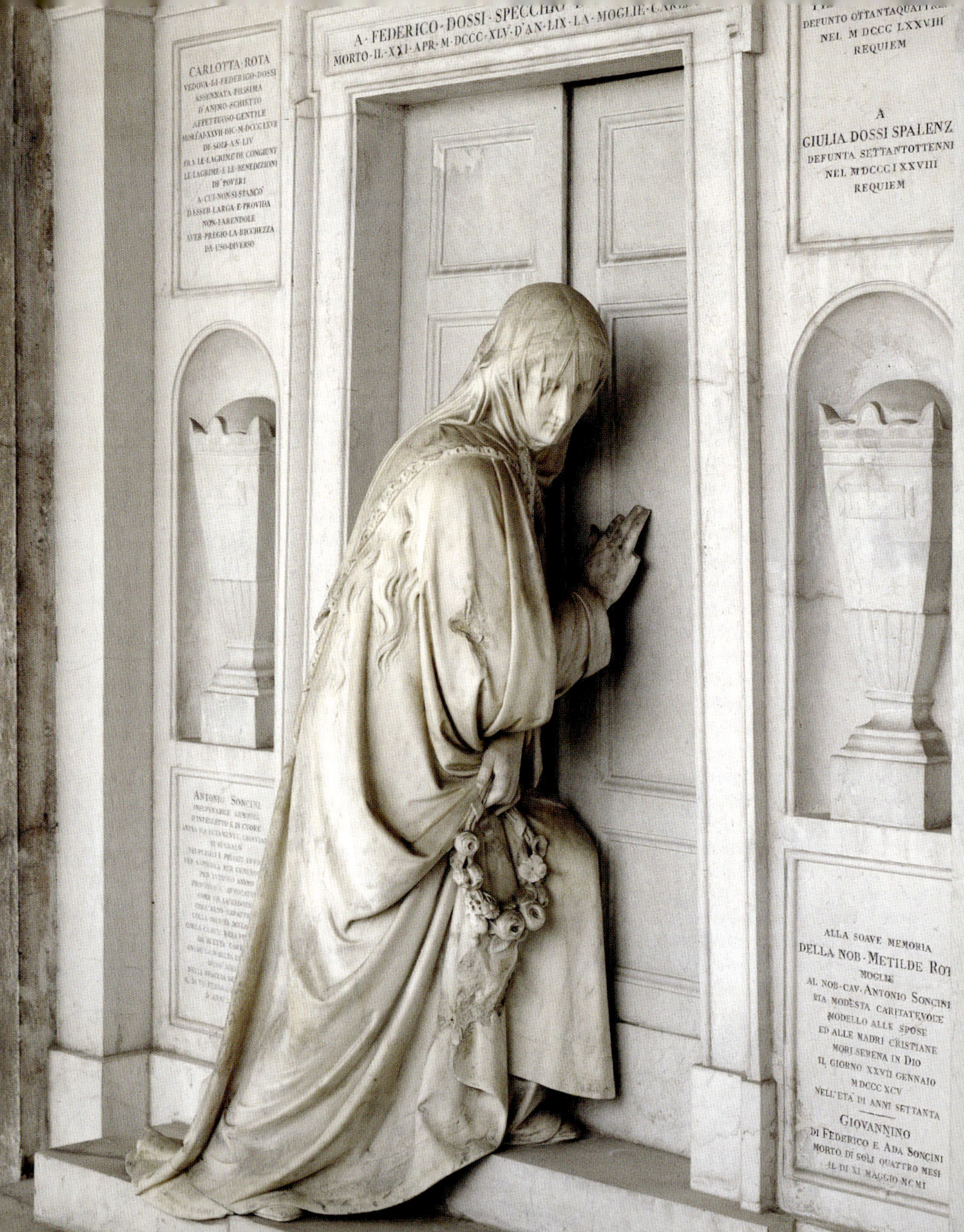

CARLOTTA·ROTA
VEDOVA·DI·FEDERICO·DOSSI
ASSENNATA·PIISSIMA
D'ANIMO·SCHIETTO
AFFETTUOSO·GENTILE
MORÌ·AI·XXVII·DIC·M·DCCCLXVII
DI·SOLI·AN·LIV
FRA·LE·LAGRIME·DE·CONGIUNTI
LE·LAGRIME·E·LE·BENEDIZIONI
DI·POVERI
A·CUI·NON·SI·STANCÒ
D'ESSER·LARGA·E·PROVIDA
NON·FARENDOLE
AVER·PREGIO·LA·RICCHEZZA
DA·USO·DIVERSO

A·FEDERICO·DOSSI·SPECCHIO
MORTO·IL·XXI·APR·M·DCCC·XLV·D'AN·LIX·LA·MOGLIE·CARLOTTA

DEFUNTO OTTANTAQUATTRENNE
NEL M DCCC LXXVIII
REQUIEM

A
GIULIA DOSSI SPALENZ
DEFUNTA SETTANTOTTENNI
NEL MDCCCLXXVIII
REQUIEM

ALLA SOAVE MEMORIA
DELLA NOB·METILDE ROI
MOGLIE
AL NOB·CAV·ANTONIO SONCINI
PIA MODESTA CARITATEVOLE
MODELLO ALLE SPOSE
ED ALLE MADRI CRISTIANE
MORÌ SERENA IN DIO
IL GIORNO XXVII GENNAIO
MDCCCXCV
NELL'ETÀ DI ANNI SETTANTA
——
GIOVANNINO
DI FEDERICO E ADA SONCINI
MORTO DI SOLI QUATTRO MESI
IL DI XI MAGGIO MCMI

Appendix

1. René Magritte
Le Faux Miroir
(*The False Mirror*), 1929
Oil on canvas, 54 x 81 cm
Museum of Modern Art,
New York

2. Maurits Cornelis Escher
Hand met spiegelende bol
(*Hand with reflecting globe*)
(detail), 1935
Lithograph, 31.8 x 21.3 cm
M.C. Escher Foundation,
Baarn

3. Maurits Cornelis Escher
Eye, 1946
Half-tone, 15.1 x 20.3 cm
M.C. Escher Foundation,
Baarn

4. Bartolomé Esteban Murillo
Self-Portrait, 1670-75
Oil on canvas, 122 x 107 cm
National Gallery, London

5. Adolphe-Jean-François Dallemagne
Unidentified Painter, 1866
Photograph, cm 10.5 x 6
Musée d'Orsay, Paris

6. Pere Borrell del Caso
Escapando de la critica
(*Fleeing the critics*), 1874
Oil on canvas, 76 x 62 cm
Banco de España, Madrid

7. Gian Lorenzo Bernini
Bust of Gabriele Fonseca,
1663-70
Marble, height 72 cm
San Lorenzo in Lucina,
Fonseca chapel, Rome

8. Gian Lorenzo Bernini
Cardinals from the Cornaro family, 1647-52
Polychrome marble
Santa Maria della Vittoria,
Cornaro chapel, Rome

9. Agostino Tassi and Orazio Gentileschi
*Ceiling of the main hall
in Palazzo Rospigliosi-Pallavicini*, 1610-12
Fresco
Palazzo Rospigliosi-Pallavicini,
Rome

10. Bramante
*Apse of the church
of Santa Maria presso
San Satiro*, 1482-86
Wall decoration
Church of Santa Maria presso
San Satiro, Milan

11. Francesco Borromini
*Perspective Gallery at Palazzo
Spada*, *circa* 1630-50
Palazzo Spada, Rome

12. Paolo Veronese
*Sequence of rooms in Villa
Barbaro*, *circa* 1560-61
Fresco
Villa Barbaro, Maser

13. Paolo Veronese
*Trompe l'oeil door with young
hunter* (detail in the last room
in the east wing),
circa 1560-61
Fresco
Villa Barbaro, Maser

14. Andrea Mantegna
San Marco, 1448-49
Tempera on canvas,
82 x 63.7 cm
Städelsches Kunstinstitut,
Frankfurt

15. El Greco
The Holy Face, circa 1580
Oil on canvas, 51 x 66 cm
Private collection, New York

16 a, b. Jan van Eyck
Annunciation, circa 1435
Oil on wood, each panel
measures 38.8 x 23.2 cm
Museo Thyssen-Bornemisza,
Madrid

17. Roger van der Weyden
Madonna with Child
(*Madonna Durán*), 1435-40
Oil on wood, 99.5 x 50.4 cm
Museo Nacional del Prado,
Madrid

18. Jean-Marie Faverjon
Trompe-l'oeil Self-Portrait,
circa 1868
Pastel, 56.5 x 46.5 cm
Musée d'Orsay, Paris

**19. Jean-Baptiste
Perroneau**
*Portrait of Jean-Baptiste
Oudry*, 1753
Oil on canvas, 131 x 105 cm
Musée du Louvre, Paris

20. Gerrit Dou
Self-Portrait, circa 1650
Oil on wood, 48 x 37 cm
Rijksmuseum, Amsterdam

21. Parmigianino
Self-Portrait in the Mirror,
1523
Oil on wood hemisphere,
diameter 24.4 cm
Kunsthistorisches Museum,
Vienna

22. *Fresco in the Villa
of Poppaea in Oplontis*,
mid 1st century AD
Wall decoration
Excavations of Oplontis, Villa
of Poppaea, Torre Annunziata

23. Juan Sánchez Cotán
*Still-life with cabbage, melon
and cucumber*, ante 1603
Oil on canvas, 68.9 x 84.5 cm
San Diego Museum of Art,
San Diego

24. Carlo Carrà
Still-life with set-square, 1917
Oil on canvas, 45 x 60 cm
Civico Museo di Arte
Contemporanea, Milan

25. Anonymous
Trompe-l'oeil, 18th century
Drawing and watercolour,
47.5 x 38 cm
Bibliothèque de l'École
Nationale des Ponts
et Chaussées, Paris

26. Anonymous
Plan for four maps,
18th century
Drawing and watercolour,
56 x 45 cm
Bibliothèque de l'École
Nationale des Ponts
et Chaussées, Paris

27. Antonio Forbera
Painter's easel, 1686
Oil on canvas,
161.5 x 94.5 cm
Musée Calvet, Avignon

28. René Magritte
La Condition humaine
(*The Human Condition*), 1933
Oil on canvas, 100 x 81 cm
National Gallery of Art,
Washington, Gift of the
Collectors Committee

29. Luciano Laurana
Ideal city, circa 1470
Tempera on wood,
67.5 x 239.5 cm
Galleria Nazionale
delle Marche, Urbino

30. Second life
Sistine Chapel

31. Second life
Virtual tunnel

32. *Unswept floor*,
1st century AD
Mosaic from Vigna Lupi
Vatican Museums,
Museo Gregoriano Profano
Vatican City

33. Daniel Spoerri
*Seville Series no. 4 and no.
12*, 1991
German (Berlin) dishes on
Sanachrome with skull and
false 50-franc note signed
by Combas, eaten by Robert
Combas and guests at the
Seville banquet,
80 x 160 x 40 cm
Atelier rue du Retrait, Paris

34. Daniel Spoerri
Seville Series no. 3 and no. 6,
1991
Dessert, Heimberger-(Anker)
dishes. Eaten by the guests
of Edith Talman and by the
designer of the dishes,
80 x 160 x 40 cm
Ueberstorf

35. Vik Muniz
Sisyphus, After Tiziano –
Pictures of Junk, 2005
Digital print, 229 x 178 cm
Gian Enzo Sperone, New York

36. Vik Muniz
Narcissus, After Caravaggio –
Pictures of Junk, 2005
Digital print
Gian Enzo Sperone, New York

37. Domenico Remps (?)
Little shop of curiosities,
second half of the 17th
century
Oil on canvas,
98.3 x 135.3 cm
Museo dell'Opificio
delle Pietre Dure, Florence

38. *Petronella Dortman's*
doll house, *circa* 1675
Various woods, mother of
pearl, tin, glass, marble, paper,
copper, stone, silk, velvet,
255 x 189.5 x 78 cm
Rijksmuseum, Amsterdam

39. Giuseppe Maria Crespi
Shelves with music books,
circa 1725
Oil on canvas
Civico Museo Bibliografico
Musicale, Bologna

40. *Wood inlay from Federico*
da Montefeltro's study,
15th century
Wood inlay
Palazzo Ducale, Urbino

41. Gianfranco Baruchello
The Big Library
(full view and detail),
1976-1986
Assemblage, various media
in wood and glass showcase,
200 x 210 x 15 cm
Fondazione Baruchello, Rome

42. Pieter von Balthasar
Wall paper mimesis, 2007
Vintage wallpaper, showcases,
exotic insects, 20 x 27 cm
Private collection

43. Pieter von Balthasar
Wall paper mimesis, 2007
Vintage wallpaper, showcases,
exotic insects, 20 x 27 cm
Private collection

44. Banksy
Sweep at Hoxton, *circa* 2001
Painting on the wall
Hoxton

45. Michelangelo
Pistoletto
Man repairing a truck, 1967
Photographic transfer on
tissue paper applied to mirror-
finish stainless steel,
230 x 120 cm
Sonnabend Gallery, Paris

46. Julian Beever
Madrid, 2007
Chalk drawing on street
Madrid

47. Domenico Ghirlandaio
Stories of John the Baptist,
Visitation (detail), 1485-90
Fresco
Santa Maria Novella,
Tornabuoni chapel, Florence

48. William Cochran
A handful of keys
Paint on marble
Great Neck, New York

49. Duane Hanson
Housewife, 1969-70
Fibreglass sculpture,
112 x 90 x 155 cm
Astrup Fearnley Collection,
Oslo

50. Duane Hanson
Homeless, 1991
Mixed media, height 168 cm
Kunsthalle, Hamburg

51. Richard Estes
Broad Street NYC, 2003
Oil on wood, 55.5 x 50.8 cm
Bettina Dotta Collection,
Montecarlo

52. Richard Haas
Crossroads Building, Times
Square, New York City, 1980
Painted Facade
New York

53. Richard Estes
Times Square, 2004
Oil on canvas, 94 x 162.6 cm
Private collection, Lisbon

Selected Bibliography

P. Larousse, "Trompe-l'œil" in *Grand Dictionnaire universel du XIXe siècle*, Paris 1866-77

M. Battersby, *Trompe l'oeil: The Eye Deceived*, New York 1974

K. Davies, *Painting Sharp Focus Still-Lifes: Trompe l'oeil Techniques*, New York 1975

M.-L. D'Otrange Mastai, *Illusion in Art: A history of pictorial illusionism*, New York 1975

J. Baudrillard, *Le Trompe-l'œil*, Urbino 1977

M. Milman, *Architectures peintes en trompe-l'œil*, Geneva 1986

M. Milman, *Le Trompe-l'œil: les illusions de la réalité*, Geneva 1992

R. Haas, B. Dunlop, *The City Is My Canvas*, Munich 2001

S. Ebert-Schifferer (edited by), *Deceptions and Illusions*, Washington 2002

M. Monestier, *Le Trompe-l'œil contemporain: Les Maîtres du Réalisme*, Paris 2002

E. Hollmann, J. Tesch, *A Trick of the Eye: Trompe l'oeil Masterpieces*, Munich 2004

M. Milman, P. Magali, R. Taws, J. Rosen, *Le trompe-l'oeil: Plus vrai que nature?*, Paris 2005

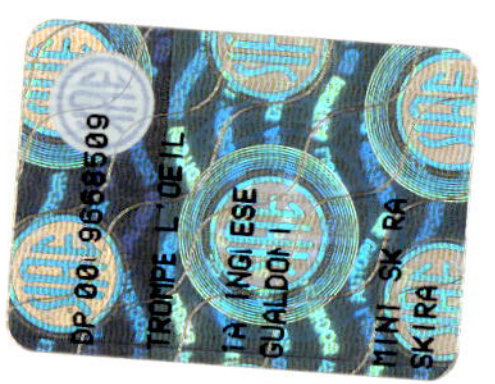

DP 00 9668509
TROMPE L'OEIL
LA INGLESE
GUALDONI
MINI SKIRA
SKIRA